I love how Dena Dyer and Tina Samples have taken these stories of wounded women in the Bible and have fleshed out such vivid pictures for us of their raw emotions—as if we know them personally. This book is filled with surprisingly fresh insights and transparent applications both from the lives of the authors and others who have also been wounded. Any woman with emotional scars— and we all have them—will be blessed by reading it. And I believe women will find here a safe place for healing as they reach out to their Jehovah-Rapha Healer and embrace new friendships with these wounded women of the Bible.

—REBECCA BARLOW JORDAN
best-selling author of eleven books, including *Day-votions® for Women, Day-votions® for Mothers*, and *Day-votions® for Grandmothers*

From the moment I saw the title, I knew this was a book that has been waiting to be written. Thankfully, it was penned by two women who have known their own waves of suffering, felt the lingering wounds left in the wake, and experienced the healing that comes from the Savior who identifies with us, cries with us, pulls us out of despair, and heals us. You'll meet women of the Bible and women among us who—though centuries apart—have shared similar heartaches. Their fascinating stories point the way to comfort, hope, and wholeness. Think of this book as a companion as you journey from whatever heartache may be holding you back, to freedom, health, and a deeper, more profound joy than you ever dreamed possible.

—BECKY JOHNSON
best-selling author, coauthor, or collaborator of more than forty books

In *Wounded Women of the Bible*, authors Dena Dyer and Tina Samples bring to life women of the Bible whose stories may be well known but at times misunderstood or underestimated. By weaving these biblical stories together with modern-day women's issues, readers will come away with a fresh perspective and a deeper appreciation for these wounded women of the Bible—as well as practical tips for dealing with their own issues today.

—KATHI MACIAS
multi-award-winning author of forty books, including *Mothers of the Bible Speak to Mothers of Today*

How many wounded women do I know personally? Do I even know one woman who has not faced some sort of heartache? *Wounded Women of the Bible* will tug on the heartstrings of every reader, offering hope and healing to the brokenhearted.

—KAREN JORDAN
author, speaker, writing instructor

Wounded Women of the Bible

Finding Hope When Life Hurts

Dena Dyer & Tina Samples

Kregel Publications

To my sweet, godly friends and prayer partners,
who have walked with me through many wounds.
I love you dearly and give thanks for you.
Dena Dyer

To all of those women who have been deeply wounded
and have no idea what to do with the wound—this book is for you.
May it touch the deepest part of your wound and bring
healing beyond your understanding.
Tina Samples

Contents

Introduction

TINA ✖ As a child, I didn't know much about the Bible. When we occasionally attended church, I heard the familiar song, "Jesus Loves Me," but never really understood its meaning. I couldn't recite John 3:16 like most children can today. I don't remember playing with other kids in Sunday school or learning Bible stories. I don't remember hearing many stories of Jesus, or even learning much about His life or death.

What I do remember is being a lonely little girl, without a home, traveling to far-off places. With so many siblings, I took turns squeezing into the front seat of our old pickup truck, while the rest of my brothers and sisters lay in the back of the camper. While we traveled I sat on my mother's lap, learning to sing. In the midst of our family's problems and difficulties, my mother taught me to sing. She swept me up in her arms and pulled me close to her warm body. "Now listen," she would say before breaking into her deep alto. Beautiful music streamed from her lips. "Sing with me. You can do it!" Before long, I was singing the tune. I was only six at the time, but eventually learned to hold the melody while she danced around it with harmony. In our sad little world, she found something worth singing about.

Fast forward ten years and picture the two of us standing before a church, singing the same song. I can still sing the song today, only this time its meaning resonates through my heart and soul. Little did I know as a small child that my mother's song was a cry of hope, strength, and faith. I reflect back on its lyrics and out bursts emotions of loneliness, the need for a friend, and carrying heavy burdens. But the writer con-cluded one thing my mother endeared to her own heart—a realization God had been searching for her all of her life. He was the perfect friend, provider, strength giver, and burden crusher. She realized in every day of her life, through every tear and sorrow, God would be there—He would not falter, waver, or tire.

Now, I realize my mother sang this during some of her darkest days. This was her hope, that though burdened and heavy laden, she could depend on God. She declared that whatever tomorrow brought, she would not face it alone; she would face it with God. My mother had reason to groan. She experienced sorrow and heartache on a daily basis. But today, she will tell you God brought something special into her life each and every day. It was a message a young girl wouldn't understand until she grew up.

A while back, the Lord brought me through an extremely difficult time. My heart ached and seeped, a wound difficult to explain. As oth-ers heard about the incident, women from the church I attended pulled me aside to share their story. At first it comforted me that others opened up about their own personal wounding. However, over time, so many stepped forward that it became overwhelming. I started counting the women—from one little church in one small town. In the final count, thirty-five women confessed to me, "That's my story." I realized I wasn't alone in my suffering, and my wounding wasn't just for me. I realized that God's plan to work in my life, and my family's life, had a broad scope; He wanted to bring healing to others facing the same issues.

Ladies, perhaps you never grew up in church or spent much time reading the Bible. Maybe you've always felt you could never relate to anyone in the Bible, and you've carried a wound that made you feel alone. I'm here to tell you that women in the Bible were wounded like you've been. Their wounds were similar to the wounds suffered by me, my mother, and even the women of one small church. Thank you for being willing to journey with us through the wounds of women in the

Bible, as well as the wounds of other women in today's world. You might find yourself saying, "That's my story." Our prayer is that you come away with greater clarity about God's love for you, as well as His healing power for your hurting heart. May you find His passion to give you hope in all things, and be assured of His desire to free you. He, too, has a song to sing over you—a song of courage, adoration, and love.

DENA ✺ When Tina called me and told me about the idea our Lord had given her, and that she wanted me to work on the book with her, I immediately thought, *yes!*

We had been friends, prayer partners, and kindred spirits for years, and had prayed for quite some time about a project we could tackle together. And when I heard the title, I knew it was a book that needed to be written.

How sweet of the Lord to give us such a rich, timely subject!

Tina and I have had very different lives. However, between the two of us, we've experienced many of the wounds suffered by the biblical women we studied. We've also seen God use excruciating wounds to purify, mold, and shape us into more resilient, hopeful believers.

My second thought after hearing the book idea from Tina was, *how in the world are we going to do this?* At the time, we lived eight hours apart. I was working a full-time job, as well as editing and writing a few hours a week. Tina worked as a music therapist and worship leader, as well as a minister's wife. We both had husbands with demanding jobs, two sons who needed attention, and other various responsibilities.

My third thought was, *Oh, no!* God always teaches me so much about any subject I write about. I knew that I would go through emotional turmoil while reflecting on my testimony, as well as stories from other wounded women.

However, God made it clear that this book was His from the start, and He would take care of us as we delved into the lives of wounded women. Somehow, we found pockets of time to write. Our families supported us and made it possible for us to dive deeply into a tough subject, and the Lord sustained us through prayer, His presence, and the comfort we received as we read His Word.

You'll hear us say it often in these pages, but I have to say it here first: He is so, so faithful. Through this process, God not only deepened our friendship, but He deepened our faith in Him. And He heightened our appreciation of His Word. We saw, like never before, that "all Scripture is God-breathed and is useful for teaching, rebuking, correcting and training in righteousness, so that the servant of God may be thoroughly equipped for every good work" (2 Tim. 3:16–17).

We understand that each reader will come to this book at a different point in her faith (and life) journey. For those who desire it, we've included a study guide at the back of the book. It can be used alone, with a friend, or in a group.

Our heartfelt prayer is that while reading the stories we've shared in *Wounded Women of the Bible*—and reflecting on what God may long to teach you in regard to your own wounds—you would find His peace for your pain, His joy in the midst of your trials, and His hope for your heartache.

1

Two Women in Solomon's Court

From Friend to Foe

❦ 1 Kings 3:16–28 ❦

WHAT DO YOU THINK of when you hear the word *friend*? Be honest. Do you think of girls' night out and envision several of your closest gal pals gabbing and laughing while eating enormous amounts of cheese dip? Or does your chest seize up a little because you've been wounded by the women you've allowed yourself to get close to?

For the two of us, Dena and Tina, our experience as friends has been wonderful. We met at an audition for a musical production, and we immediately felt as if we'd known one another forever. Our husbands were both students at a local seminary, we both loved to sing and act, and we both loved the Lord. We just clicked right away. Over a decade later, one of us lives in Texas and one resides in Colorado, but we have the sort of friendship where we can go without talking for ages, and then when we call one another, we pick right up. We are truly "soul sisters."

Sadly, though, not all of our friendships have been wonderful. Some have been painful experiences. We've both been in ministry for many years, and we've been terribly hurt by fellow Christian women. And we'll admit that we've done our fair share of hurting others as well.

Ladies, we're not the first to experience our particular wounds. Even in biblical times, there were mishaps in friendships, tensions between women, and betrayals of all kinds. In the book of 1 Kings, two women's lives intersected in a way that would forever change them. In the midst of their "friendship" journey, something went terribly wrong. See if you can relate, even just a bit, to their story.

TINA ❧ The young woman rose in the night, still weary from the stress of giving birth. Her baby's cries echoed throughout the room. "Come here, little one," she murmured as she pulled the child next to her warm body and began feeding him. She tugged at the blankets, tucking them gently around the infant to form a cocoon. Her tired lids drooped, and her heavy head drifted side to side.

Eventually, the fight for sleep became too much and she surrendered. The weight of her body slid to the hard ground, and she nestled next to her warm child. The moon glistened and the twinkling stars seemed to keep time with the singing of the crickets. Hours passed. Restless in the night, the woman rolled her drained body onto her baby, never realizing what lay beneath her.

When she finally woke, she found her child's face muzzled against her body. "No, no, no!" she cried; her trembling hands cupped his small frame as she moved swiftly to untangle the lifeless body. She vigorously rubbed the side of her baby's face and huddled over him, rocking back and forth. "Breathe, please," she pleaded. Dazed and confused, she held tight, pulling the baby to her chest. Her tears fell, pouring onto the body that lay limp in her arms.

In the midst of her pain and loss, she rose from her position and entered the area where her friend slept.

Did she go to wake her and then unexpectedly change her mind?

As her eyes fell upon the living child resting next to her friend, longing and passion stirred her heart. Quietly, cautiously, she placed her deceased child next to her friend. Without hesitation, she lifted the living child to her chest and claimed it as her own.

Was the mother of the dead child driven by exhaustion? Had grief forced her to make such a shocking move? We don't know her motives, but her story will forever touch our hearts.

Though most people focus on the loss of the living child and the wisdom of Solomon in this story, I want to speak about the wound between the two women. A woman will endure many wounds in her lifetime, but the betrayal of a friend is one of the most difficult to overcome. Why? God created women to need other women. Our hearts beat in tune with one another, our minds function much the same, and we're easily woven together—like threads in a tapestry.

Haven't you noticed that something magical happens when women gather? The air becomes thick with chatter. The room fills with laughter. Everything comes alive. *We* come alive! We need female connection and spiritual union.

As a young girl, I moved around quite a bit. It was one of the loneliest kinds of adventures a child endures. We almost never stayed in one place long enough for any of us to make friends, but when we finally settled down during my middle school years, I found a friend with whom I could laugh, spend time, and enjoy life. For the first time, I experienced what it felt like to have a true friend.

God often brings us those much-needed companions at just the right time. Perhaps their role will not be "best friend," but they will be the neighbor that provides us with hospitality, the mentor from a Bible study, or the one we sit next to at church every Sunday morning. Perhaps that friend will be someone we only see at work, or maybe she'll be our movie friend or coffee buddy. Maybe the friendship runs deeper, and she will become our prayer partner or the one we run to when we are hurting. And if she's the one we share our deepest desires and secrets with, then she's a rare jewel indeed.

Strong Bond

First Kings 3 speaks of two women who shared a common bond. They were both prostitutes, pregnant at the same time. And prostitutes or not, they were women with real emotions and concerns. Though not much is said about them, there is one important fact that stands out in Scripture—they lived together in the same house. And because of that, it is fair to assume they were more than acquaintances. They most certainly found a way to visit, share about their day, and cook and clean together. There must have been a bond between the two.

Imagine sharing a house with another woman with both of you pregnant! That in itself is enough to bring about a significant attachment. And of course, there was much to talk about—whether they wanted to raise a boy or a girl, what kind of mother they'd like to become, and what they might name the children. Perhaps they sewed clothes, made blankets, and in other ways readied themselves for the arrival of their babies.

The two women also experienced something that most contemporary women will never share: they delivered each other's babies. Picture that moment when two babies, days apart, are brought into the world. What joy and life must have filled the home. They walked with one another for nine months through their pregnancies, and then helped bring new lives into the world together. Their willingness to fight over the living child indicates that the babies were wanted, treasured; to be childless was to be cursed of God. The two must have shared a glorious moment of celebration.

Soon, however, these two women who shared their home, their lives, and their pregnancies came face-to-face with devastating wounds—one from an accident and the other from a deliberate, hurtful act.

At some point during the night, one young woman lay on her child and smothered him to death. It was a tragedy—with pain beyond our understanding. What would bring that woman to take her child into her friend's room and exchange babies with her? She left her lifeless child there and claimed the living one as her own.

Grief causes us to do strange things.

Transparency—Difficult to Find?

Why is it difficult for us to be transparent? For some reason, we find it easier to lie and deceive one another rather than speak openly from the heart. We may even abandon our friend, shunning them without speaking a word.

Why was it difficult for the woman who lost her child to go to the other and weep in her arms? She could have unburdened herself, honestly crying out, "My child is dead!" The outcome would have been so different, with no wall of betrayal between them. I believe the woman whose child still lived would have embraced the one who had accidentally killed her own baby. She too had carried a child and understood how it felt to be a mother.

A while back, my husband and I went through a difficult time at our church. Though the issue involved my husband, I was attached to him and people could not separate the two of us. In the process, many women who had been my friends abandoned me. Rather than embracing me with love and grace as Christ would have done, they turned away. I desired to sit across from them and listen as they shared their deepest wounds about what had happened. Perhaps they struggled, as I did, to sort out their feelings. But instead of being transparent with me, they found it easier to walk away without speaking to me, leaving me in a puddle of pain.

While grieving and trying to work through my own hurt concerning the issue, I ended up having to endure the sorrow from losing friends whom I had confided in, trusted, and loved. What I needed most was an understanding friend. On my face to the Lord in tears, I cried out. My soul and heart groaned in grief. "Why, Lord?" I cried. "All I ever tried to do was love them!" I felt betrayed that they could abandon me so quickly, filling their hearts with bitterness toward me. The wound was deep and lasting.

The Wound

The next morning the other woman rose from her sleep, gently reached for her child to nurse him, and then realized that something was terribly wrong.

"My child!" she screamed, as she held the lifeless baby in her arms.

In that instant, the two women shared another common experience. Both felt the sting of grief. They both understood how it felt to lose a child.

Frightened and terrified, the woman jumped up, kicking the covers to the side. Her heart raced as she ran toward the window. "Help me!" she gasped, sobbing.

As the mother moved from the dark shadows and into the morning light, a warm ray of sunshine fell upon the baby's silken skin. Suddenly, the light revealed something the darkness had hidden. The baby she held was not hers. Bewildered, she quickly ran to the other woman— only to find her own child in the arms of her friend.

"That's my child!" she cried, reaching for him.

Her "friend" quickly turned away. Clutching the infant tightly, she declared, "No! The child is mine!"

Envision the woman, draped in sorrow and pain, standing before her friend. Imagine what she might have thought or felt: *How could you? Why would you do such a thing? Why would you hurt me like this?* We have said similar words, and felt the same.

Sisters, God created us to be lovely beings. Women are gorgeous, striking, and captivating. He delights in us in every way. His print is strongly embedded in the creation of who we are. But along with our

God-given beauty, we also have a fleshly, willful side. We have strong opinions, feelings that are easily hurt, and a talent for holding grudges. We can become selfish, self-centered, and self-seeking. And, like the two women, we have a desire to protect ourselves from isolation, loneliness, and cultural prejudices. Every woman who has experienced that fleshly side, or who has had to face it from another woman, understands its impact.

Our minds are powerful tools. They can drive us to hurt others, cast them aside, and betray them. We rationalize our actions and create our own version of reality: *This is right! This is the truth!* In her mind, the mother who lost her child had decided that the child she now held was hers.

Healing Justice

The case of *Mother v. Mother* eventually ended up before a judge. They entered King Solomon's court. He was one of the wisest kings who ever ruled Israel.

The mother whose child was taken immediately pleaded her case:

> "Pardon me, my lord. This woman and I live in the same house, and I had a baby while she was there with me. The third day after my child was born, this woman also had a baby. We were alone; there was no one in the house but the two of us.
>
> "During the night this woman's son died because she lay on him. So she got up in the middle of the night and took my son from my side while I your servant was asleep. She put him by her breast and put her dead son by my breast. The next morning, I got up to nurse my son—and he was dead! But when I looked at him closely in the morning light, I saw that it wasn't the son I had borne."

The other woman said, "No! The living one is my son; the dead one is yours."

But the first one insisted, "No! The dead one is yours; the living one is mine." And so they argued before the king. (1 Kings 3:17–22)

Their response to one another is similar to the ways we treat each other. But the Lord gave Solomon great wisdom, and he determined the truth. He ordered that the living child be cut in half, with one half given to each of the mothers. The child's real mother made herself known by her deep love, shouting in surrender, "Give her the living baby! Don't kill him!"

In the end, the right woman got her child back, and justice was served. But the situation is heartbreaking. Who knows what happened to the relationship between the two women? Some might say that the wound was too deep to mend. Others may say that a true friend would offer forgiveness.

When we have been betrayed by someone we have trusted, it *hurts*. The hurt runs deeply through our veins and attaches itself like a tight-fitting glove. It's not easily removed. The pain is ever-present and strong. I've never met a woman who hasn't been hurt by another woman at some point in her life. In fact, I've spent countless hours praying and crying with women who have been deeply hurt by other women.

So why keep pursuing this thing called friendship? God didn't create us to desire friendships just so we could risk our hearts and then get pummeled by those who take advantage of us. Instead, He created us to crave friends, to be drawn in by fellowship. Through that amazing connection, we see Christ in ways we have not; we learn more about Him and about ourselves; and we learn to lean on Him in the midst of the trials and joys those relationships bring. Through that "heartstring" tie with another, we come to a larger understanding of the power of love: "Greater love has no one than this: to lay down one's life for one's friends" (John 15:13). That is the power of friendship.

We have to remember: we can't see what God sees, we don't know what God knows, and we have no idea how God will deal with any given situation. But we can rest in the assurance of Psalm 56:8: "You keep track of all my sorrows. You have collected all my tears in your bottle. You have recorded each one in your book" (NLT). Psalm 147:3 says, "He heals the brokenhearted and binds up their wounds."

God will restore us, in due time.

In my own life, the Lord sent women to hold my hand during that difficult time at church. Though I lost many relationships with women I'd considered friends, others endured. Instead of turning away, they gently walked beside me and placed their arms around me. They embraced me with phone calls, cards, and emails. They embraced me with love, warmth, and prayers. They embraced me with grace.

And the Lord revealed something to me: *These are your true friends, Tina.* They were the friend Christ would have been to me, had He been here in the flesh. I am grateful for those true friendships, and I am grateful that Christ opened my eyes to see them.

DENA ❦ When "Jules" called me and asked me to go shopping with her, I was thrilled. Though our husbands worked together, I had seen her as unreachable. Jules—younger, financially well-off, and beautiful—seemed like someone I couldn't relate to. I had never expected her to reach out to me.

But we had a great time shopping. From there, our friendship grew. We became buddies, then confidantes, and finally, prayer partners. Other friends of mine had recently found themselves overwhelmed with job and/or family responsibilities, and I was hungry for a girlfriend to share life with.

I'd often felt like the "giver" in my relationships, the one doing all the calling and pursuing, because I valued friendship with other women and made friends a priority. But Jules sought me out, bought me little gifts, and made sure I felt included when she had social gatherings. She freely gave her time, affection, and words of encouragement.

I ignored the warning signs, of course, and put Jules on a pedestal that she never should have been on (I'm bad about that). At the time, I didn't see her faults. And I sure didn't own up to mine.

A Friendship Dies

And then it happened. Jules suffered a terrible loss, and all of a sudden, she shut me out. No more phone calls, no more shopping trips, nothing. Nada. Nil. Zip.

At first, I was confused. Later, I felt offended. And finally, after I heard about blatantly false things she told others about my husband and me, I got angry. In fact, I became livid and could barely speak of her—for months.

How dare she! I thought. After all, we were friends . . . accountability partners . . . sisters in Christ.

The wound went so deep that I couldn't speak of her without shaking. My husband tried to warn me that I was becoming bitter.

Never one to turn my back on a good grudge, I didn't dispute his claims. But I also wasn't about to give up on my righteous (I thought) indignation. I had trusted Jules. I had shared my life, my intimate thoughts, and my prayers with her.

It was, to put it simply, devastating.

One of the hardest parts of the whole situation was that Jules never owned up to any of her actions. Not once did she say, "I'm sorry" or even explain either the distance she put between us or the hurtful actions she took.

And like that mother whose child was taken, I felt something had been taken from me: my expectations of what a friendship should be. I, too, grieved.

I'm not proud to say it, but it took years before my chest didn't feel as if it were seizing up at the mention of Jules. I tried to just put her out of my mind. I even tried to pray for her a few times. But it felt false. What I really wanted to do was pray like the psalmists, who—at times—asked for God to smite their enemies and bring destruction upon them.

My anger frustrated my husband. And to be honest, I was disappointed in myself. I loved Jesus. I knew He asked me to forgive. Hadn't He forgiven His enemies, even those who put Him to death?

I knew I needed to obey. But my "want to" was stuck.

Gradually, the thought began to sink in that I was only holding myself hostage by clutching the things I'd suffered to my chest as if they were trophies. I was keeping myself from new friendships God might want to give, because I was terribly afraid of being hurt again.

And so during a weekend retreat, after months of putting off doing what I knew I should do, I sobbed and asked God's forgiveness for holding onto anger and bitterness. I asked Him to help my emotions follow my actions, and I forgave my "enemy." I completely turned Jules over to God.

"Bless her, Lord," I prayed.

And—miraculously—I really, truly meant it.

Since then, though I haven't pursued a relationship with Jules, I've seen her through more compassionate eyes (funny how God changes us when we obey Him). I can look back on the past and see how things might have felt from Jules's perspective. Like Tina said, grief makes people do strange things.

Heidi's Story

Sometimes our own grief causes others to say and do strange things when they are around us. Recently, my friend "Heidi" shared her experience about that particular brand of disappointment and betrayal:

Brenda and I were in the same Sunday school class and our friendship just blossomed. I had been so wounded by my own mother's rejection of me that her friendship fed my soul.

Brenda and I became inseparable. My little boys called her Auntie. We talked for hours about any and every thing.

I had not realized how much trust had become an issue to me until I let go and entrusted her with my deepest struggles. She encouraged me and spoke God's truth into the dark places of my soul. Having grown up as an Army brat, I had never experienced long-lasting friendships. As a teenager, I lost my dad to cancer and was abandoned by my mom. I clung to the Lord for dear life. In the years that followed, I began to see God redeem those losses. My friendship—my sisterhood—with Brenda felt like part of that redeeming. I had found a friend who chose to call me family, and it was profound.

In the context of this joy, I never saw it coming: a wounding that cut to my core. My trusted friend sat across from me and passionately expressed her newfound belief that healing comes to anyone who has enough faith. My heart sunk, and I took a deep breath and asked, "So, Brenda, are you saying that if a believer is sick and prays but isn't healed, it's because that believer lacked faith?"

I silently begged for the answer I hoped she would give.

"Yes! That's exactly what I'm saying. As believers, if we have enough faith, then we receive healing!"

My mouth went dry. I tried one more time to clarify: "This is hard for me. So, are you saying that you believe that my dad would not have died if only we had more faith?" Her response would either carve a deeper wound or would salvage the pain I was feeling.

"Yes. That's what I'm saying. If y'all had enough faith, your dad would have been healed and wouldn't have died."

I felt so betrayed. The door of my heart slammed shut, and the rest of the evening passed in a blur. I let her know definitively how wounding her statements were. But it fell on deaf ears and she didn't back down.

We remain friends to this day. However, due to various circumstances, we rarely see each other. I have tried to move forward with her, but I know it will never be the same. Where I once felt completely safe, I no longer do. The biggest loss of my life was blamed on my own lack of faith. It felt callous and insensitive, although I know that was not her intent. Her response to my direct questioning that night reinforced how oblivious she was to the pain she'd inflicted. She'd lost sight of my heart and all the pain about my dad's death that I had entrusted to her.

He Hurts with Us

When you experience the pain of a friend's betrayal, like Heidi or I did, you may feel as if you've been gut-punched. You wonder if you will ever be able to trust someone again.

From experience, I believe that you will . . . if you allow yourself to. Each of us needs friends, and all relationships come with risk. We may never understand how people who seemed to love us could hurt us so badly, but if we're honest with ourselves, we can begin to see how we, at times, have inflicted pain on others.

We all need God's grace—desperately.

Now, I have a question for you, whether or not you've been hurt recently or in the past: will you choose to believe that God hurts with you? That as your perfect heavenly Father, He longs to take you in His arms and hold you? One of the shortest verses in the Bible is also the most poignant: "Jesus wept" (John 11:35). As Jesus stood beside Mary and Martha at the tomb of their brother—His dear friend, Lazarus— He cried. Jesus knew He was going to raise Lazarus from the dead in mere moments. So I believe He cried not out of grief for Himself, but out of compassion and empathy. He saw the hurting friends and relatives of Lazarus, and His heart broke because He loved them so completely.

He sees our hurts, hears our cries, and feels our pain. In Luke 4:18–19, Jesus affirms that a large part of His purpose was to heal our wounds: "The Spirit of the Lord is on me, because he has anointed me to proclaim good news to the poor. He has sent me to proclaim freedom for the prisoners and recovery of sight for the blind, to set the oppressed free, to proclaim the year of the Lord's favor." God understands even when things don't make sense to us: "Great is our Lord and mighty in power; his understanding has no limit" (Ps. 147:5). He is our great comforter and will rip away the tight-fitting shroud of grief that surrounds our being: "The LORD sustains the humble but casts the wicked to the ground" (v. 6).

The situation with our betrayer may not have been resolved—but we can find resolution through Christ.

If we're willing to let Him, God will bring us to a place where we can forgive—not to appease the other person, or to let the other person off the hook, but to bring healing to our own lives. He will mend our broken heart so that we can find a way to fully live.

Hopefully, one day, God will bring a true friend into our life who will stand with us, speak truth into our life, and embrace us—even in the darkest times. One who will not leave us; who will not abandon us; and who will be a friend to walk beside us, no matter what.

Whether we find that friend in our earthly lives or not, that is what Christ does for us. And whether our earthly friends stay or go, He remains steadfastly by our side.

He is, simply, the best friend we could ever have.

2

Abigail

From Abused to Adored

❧ 1 SAMUEL 25 ❧

TINA ❧ *Clang!* A loud noise of something hitting the wall and, somehow, my twelve-year-old mind understood it was a plate of food. My siblings and I heard yelling, screaming, and stammering, but none of us really understood what our father was saying. We scattered like ants do after a rock hits their mound—running into our rooms, far away from the war zone.

I could always tell what kind of mood my father would be in the moment he entered the door. Often, before he ever came close to the house, I could hear his shouting and cursing. That was my cue to run and hide. My wounds as a child were deep, but I can't imagine the wounds my mother carried.

There are many women who live with abusive relationships. Abuse can come in many different forms, and one kind of abuse is not greater than another. I sat with my friend in the emergency room, holding her trembling hands. I couldn't stop staring at the bruises around her face and the cuts on her lip. Her eyes were swollen from the tears as well as the pain. My heart burned with emotion. Her young face still radiated beauty, but did she know it? Abuse takes its toll and can strip a woman of all the lovely things God created in her. She may come to believe that she's not beautiful, worthy, or loveable. She will feel like the abuse is her fault and that she deserved it. The abuser's voice dominates her thoughts and edges out God's voice of truth.

It's not uncommon for women to become trapped in the midst of the abuse, and for the abuser to have a powerful hold upon her life. Out of fear, she will continue in the unhealthy (and sometimes dangerous) relationship without ever seeking help. What she may not understand is that God can bring healing to her life, as well as her husband's, when healthy boundaries are set. Having an alcoholic father created dysfunction within our family; because of that, I became a peacemaker. Understandably, I found myself wanting to rescue those in my family—to take control of a situation that seemed completely out of control. As I've healed, and continue to heal, from my past, I'm learning that only God is in control, and His understanding is greater than mine.

An Abusive Wound

I love the name Abigail. I always wanted a girl, but the Lord blessed me with two amazing sons. If I had a daughter, I would consider naming her Abigail. It means, "a father's joy." Don't you love that?

Abigail was, according to 1 Samuel 25:3, "an intelligent and beautiful woman." She probably lived in comfort and had everything she needed, because Scripture also mentions that Nabal, the man she married, was wealthy. Others around the village and neighborhood probably believed Abigail was happy because she lived in splendor. But we women often put up a front—showing to others only what we *want* them to see.

The truth is that Abigail lived with a "surly and mean" man. *Surly* can mean anything from simply uncivil, sullen, and brooding to outright hostile, menacing, and threatening.

One day while David and his men were in the desert, they heard that
Nabal was shearing his three thousand sheep. Nabal can be credited as
a hard worker—but his heart was as hard as a boulder.

David and his men were hiding in the desert because King Saul was
trying to kill David. In dire need of food and supplies, David sent his
men to Nabal's land to gather whatever provisions they could.

Ten young men approached on their horses and spoke boldly the
words that David asked them to say:

> "Long life to you! Good health to you and your household!
> And good health to all that is yours!
>
> "Now I hear that it is sheep-shearing time. When your
> shepherds were with us, we did not mistreat them, and the
> whole time they were at Carmel nothing of theirs was miss-
> ing. Ask your own servants and they will tell you. Therefore
> be favorable toward my men, since we come at a festive time.
> Please give your servants and your son David whatever you can
> find for them." (1 Sam. 25:6–8)

David was telling Nabal that while he and his men were in the desert, he did not mistreat any of Nabal's shepherds or his sheep—though
he probably could have taken what he wanted and left it at that. Instead,
he did an honorable thing and sent his men to ask for the provisions. He
only asked, not demanded.

Nabal's response was unkind. He had no compassion for the men
or their request. (Later on, we'll understand one reason why he may
have acted as he did.) He even insulted them by shouting, "Who is this
David? . . . Why should I take my bread and water, and the meat I have
slaughtered for my shearers, and give it to men coming from who knows
where?" (vv. 10–11).

What a mistake! When the men returned to David and told him
about Nabal's cruel response, David shouted to his men, "Put on your

swords!" and suddenly four hundred soldiers raced toward Nabal's home.

One of the servants immediately shared with Abigail what had happened:

> "David sent messengers from the wilderness to give our master his greetings, but he hurled insults at them. Yet these men were very good to us. They did not mistreat us, and the whole time we were out in the fields near them nothing was missing. Night and day they were a wall around us the whole time we were herding our sheep near them. Now think it over and see what you can do, because disaster is hanging over our master and his whole household. He is such a wicked man that no one can talk to him." (vv. 14–17)

And in that moment a wound, which many women can relate to, surfaced. Reflect on what Abigail may have felt as she received the news of what happened: embarrassment, shame, dishonor. Who knows what thoughts and fears rushed to her mind in that one second. Did her heart sink in despair as she realized they were in trouble? What wounds did she experience at that very instant? This was not the first time Nabal had been mean and hurtful—even the servants understood what kind of man they served. Abigail, herself, understood Nabel's temper. She lived with it.

My heart aches with Abigail's. My family and I have watched similar situations unfold regarding my father and how he treated others. Shame and embarrassment draped us like a canopy. At times, our suffocation felt completely unbearable.

The Bible says that Abigail lost no time and jumped right into rescue mode. She scurried to gather as many provisions as she could. She packed mounds of food and wine, and eventually sent her servants on ahead of her, telling them she wouldn't be far behind. And she did all of this without telling Nabal.

Journey to Peace

I remember when my mother shouted, "Hurry up! Your father is on his way home." We scurried to pick up, while she ran to cook and get food on the table. It wasn't easy, or even healthy, but my mother knew what to do to keep the peace in order to get us through another day.

My father and Nabal had something in common. They both drank alcohol in excess. Alcohol defined their behavior, their character, and their relationships. However, it didn't define who God created them to be. Somewhere deep within was the man God put His fingerprint upon. Sin often crowds the appearance, heart, and mind of others, and we forget that God is anywhere near . . . but He is, and His love is ever close.

Imagine beautiful Abigail riding her small donkey through a mountain ravine to meet David, when all of a sudden, she sees a huge cloud of dust descending toward her. There's David charging forth, like a ruthless warrior, with four hundred mighty soldiers.

> When Abigail saw David, she quickly got off her donkey and bowed down before David with her face to the ground. She fell at his feet and said: "Pardon your servant, my lord, and let me speak to you; hear what your servant has to say. Please pay no attention, my lord, to that wicked man Nabal. He is just like his name—his name means Fool, and folly goes with him. And as for me, your servant, I did not see the men my lord sent." (1 Sam. 25:23–25)

What I love about this biblical moment is that Abigail was honest with David about her husband and his foolish ways. What I dislike about this passage is that she took the blame for Nabal's doing. When we speak out of our wounds, we say things (honest or not) to ease the pain, still the waters, and make peace.

We all made excuses for my father's behavior and often took

responsibility for his actions, saying, "If I had just done what he said to do . . ." or "If I had only understood . . ."

It wasn't until many years later, when God began healing me, that I began to understand why we said those things. We acted out of our fear and wounds. I imagine Abigail did the same.

I also learned something about my mother during those years of healing. She carried something with her that she didn't try to hide. She expressed it openly, but I didn't recognize the secret to her endurance until I found myself suffering through trials—until I needed a way to mend my own personal wounds.

My mother understood that not by her might, not by her will, not by her doing, but by God's strength and power alone was she able to carry on. Through His strength, she was able to get up in the morning. Through His strength she was able to live and breathe. She *was* weak, but through Christ, she became so much stronger than I ever imagined.

Like He did for my mother, the Lord gave Abigail supernatural strength:

> "Since the LORD has kept you from bloodshed and from avenging yourself with your own hands, may your enemies and all who are intent on harming my lord be like Nabal. And let this gift, which your servant has brought to my lord, be given to the men who follow you.
>
> "Please forgive your servant's presumption. The LORD your God will certainly make a lasting dynasty for my lord, because you fight the LORD's battles." (vv. 26–28)

Did you see it? In the midst of those spoken words, there was a surprising revelation. Abigail asked David to forgive her husband's offenses!

Suddenly, I'm reminded of my mother's wounded heart coming before the Lord God Almighty and doing the very same. Year after year, she prayed for my father. She pleaded, she asked forgiveness—and she didn't waiver. In the midst of her suffering, she found an altar to fall before; it was there that she allowed the wounds to fall from her aching soul. And just like David heard and received Abigail's words, the Lord did the same for my mother.

> David said to Abigail, "Praise be to the LORD, the God of Israel, who has sent you today to meet me. May you be blessed for your good judgment and for keeping me from bloodshed this day and from avenging myself with my own hands. Otherwise, as surely as the LORD, the God of Israel, lives, who has kept me from harming you, if you had not come quickly to meet me, not one male belonging to Nabal would have been left alive by daybreak."
>
> Then David accepted from her hand what she had brought him and said, "Go home in peace. I have heard your words and granted your request." (vv. 32–35)

Just as Abigail left her conversation with David full of peace, my mother would rise from her deep conversations with the Lord and feel hope. She knew that the Lord had heard her words, her heart, and her despair. She also believed without a doubt that God would one day grant her request. And she knew that, in the meantime, God would be her strength and help.

> When Abigail went to Nabal, he was in the house holding a banquet like that of a king. He was in high spirits and very drunk. So she told him nothing at all until daybreak. Then in the morning, when Nabal was sober, his wife told him all these things, and his heart failed him and he became like a stone. About ten days later, the LORD struck Nabal and he died. (vv. 36–38)

Abigail, in her wisdom, knew not to approach Nabal while he was drunk. And though no one really knows what went through Nabal's mind after hearing the story of what his wife had done for him, we can guess that he was struck with some kind of illness that eventually took his life. We can also assume that he died without knowing the Lord.

After Nabal died, David took Abigail as his wife. Their initial conversation was a turning point for both of them. For me, coming to know the Lord at thirteen was a turning point. Each day as I learned all I could about my heavenly Father, I had to face my worldly father. There were times when the alcohol and abuse seemed too much to bear, and those days were extraordinarily difficult.

One day while reading my Bible, I came upon John 16:33. I remember weeping as I experienced a sense of the Lord's presence. At that very moment, God revealed to me that through Him I could have peace in all things, and that although we live in a fallen world, I could have joy through Him—because the world has no power over God.

He has overcome the world. He is the conqueror, defeater, and deliverer, and He reigns over all things. That Scripture verse carried me through my high school years, until I left home and found healing. God used it to give peace to my heart during my toughest days.

Oh yes, and this is no small thing: my earthly father came to know the God who reigns over the world. After his conversion, he never missed church on Sunday, and the Lord healed my father of his alcoholism.

My father eventually lived to give back rather than to steal. He lived to do good rather than bad. He lived to love and loved to live. He took his last breath in the presence of his family and his Holy Father, whom he had come to love with his whole heart.

DENA ❦ In Tina's family, God won out. And in Abigail's family, God won out as well. After years of living with a fool, she married a king. I really admire Abigail.

His Divine Purpose

Abigail's story is a classic example of God turning evil into good. Just as Romans 8:28 says, "in all things God works for the good of those who love him, who have been called according to his purpose." It's obvious that Abigail loved the Lord, and we know that David was called to be king. Through the foolishness of Nabal and the intelligence and beauty of Abigail, God carried out His divine purposes.

My own family's history proves that God uses everything—even the most undesirable parts of our past—for His, and our, good. I grew up with a father whose traumatic childhood affected his moods. My mother, brother, and I learned, like Tina's family, to keep the peace at all costs.

Not surprisingly, I grew up as a people-pleaser. I felt guilty if I asked a fast-food worker to repeat my order back to me. (Seriously.)

Over time, with the help of godly counseling and lots of time in God's Word, I unlearned a lot of terrible habits and thought patterns that I'd previously viewed as normal. I also made peace with my childhood. It wasn't easy—and it took years—but as an adult, I have the perspective and experiences to know how hard parenting and marriage are, and I can understand the reasons Dad had learned to process anger so destructively.

Through the years, Dad allowed the Lord to change him as well, and now he's a much softer, gentler person. I love to see him around my two boys. He's a wonderful grandparent!

It would be nice if we all grew up in homes filled with love, appropriate affection, and perfect parents. It would also be great if spouses didn't cheat, friends didn't lie, and perverts didn't prey on children.

However, as we all know, family-of-origin wounds are rampant in our society, because we live on a fallen planet. I dare say that most women will experience abuse—by a friend, boyfriend, parent, or even a child—at some point in her life. It's way too common, and it's too often debilitating.

Emotionally Abused

"Mary" suffered for years in an abusive marriage. I first met her at auditions for a performing group at the Baptist Student Union building on the Baylor campus. We were both freshmen, and we hit it off immediately. She became one of my best friends and my running partner. I really admired her. Both smart and fun, Mary was extremely dedicated to the Lord. After college, as God would have it, Mary and I both went on two-year missionary assignments—hers was overseas, and mine was in the United States—and we both met our husbands during those two years.

Sadly, Mary's marriage didn't last. She says, "My ex-husband was emotionally abusive—there were signs when we were dating that I ignored. He was controlling even then, making lists of things he didn't like about me and wanted to change. I ignored everything because he was so charming, and I had never really had a romantic relationship before."

Mary's ex—"Mike"—said he was a Christian and was called to the ministry, and after they married, he made sure everything in their home was "holy." That meant that if something was a gift from someone he considered "unholy," Mike made Mary throw it away. He began cutting her off from friends and family who didn't meet his approval.

Mike moved from job to job, sometimes not working for months or years at a time because he didn't feel "called." He became the pastor of two churches, but when things got difficult in those congregations, he became impatient with them and quit. Mary says, "The last church he worked for told Mike to resign or be fired; after that, his attitude was, 'Well, God, I tried to serve you, and you didn't help me, so I won't even bother from now on.'"

Mary had trouble conceiving, and she says, "Mike would say the worst things to me, and there was agony in my own soul too, because I also wanted children. When I finally did get pregnant and our daughter was born, it brought a lot of joy to us. However, it didn't take long before she was not meeting his standards either. He would criticize her, even when she was a small child, and he was extremely overprotective."

My friend admits, "During all this time, I struggled with my relationship to God. I was being forced to submit to my husband, who never really showed me any love at all, and I became very, very angry and withdrawn. I would go to church and even volunteer, but I was so angry at what was happening! Mike wouldn't go to church. He didn't care. I felt like I was the only one who cared for my child's spiritual growth."

Mike eventually had an affair with a student (while teaching part-time at a community college) and moved out. Mary says, "I asked him to go to counseling with me, and he did—once. I really wanted to work on our marriage, but his basic take on everything was all men have affairs, and I didn't take care of myself after the baby was born—so who could blame him?" Their divorce was final in July 2009.

Mike ended up living in his car and finally left the United States to return to his native country and live with his family. He left without saying good-bye to his daughter, "Sheree." Mary and Sheree were left to pick up the pieces . . . but all was not lost.

Mary says, "Sheree's life is completely different since her father left. Without the constant emotional abuse, she is happy, loving, and free to be who she *truly* is. She sings constantly and her teachers say she is well-adjusted."

As for Mary, she found God to be faithful in sustaining and strengthening her. She also found a new ministry that she absolutely loves. Through the single parents' class at her church, she's met other single moms and loves to babysit their kids so they can have a break. ("It gives my daughter a playmate too," she explains.) In the past year, Mary has also been blessed with the ability to buy a new house next door to her parents.

She says, "When I bought the house, I told the Lord that I would use it for Him however He wanted me to use it. For so long, I didn't use my spiritual gifts while I was married; it's nice to have them back. I've missed serving."

Life's not easy as a single mom. Mary admits that it's a daily struggle to choose to forgive. She says, "Holidays are especially hard—I really dread Christmas, to be honest, and I hope that improves with time."

She also wrestles daily with the expectations she had for her family that didn't turn out how she had planned, but she concludes that her marriage to an abusive man—and the eventual divorce—has made her a more compassionate and empathetic person.

God Is Big Enough

Perhaps the loss of a dream is one of the hardest things to get past when you've been abused. We all have expectations of our loved ones, and when they fail to live up to them, we can become angry at God and withdraw from those who do care about us.

I went through a period of severe depression after my first son was born, and I had to force myself to go to church, even though my husband was in youth ministry at the time. For a while, I quit going at all.

Looking back, I can see that all the years of emotional upheaval in my childhood home resulted in me trying to be perfect all the time, in order not to rock anyone's boat. It had become exhausting, though, and finally my own boat capsized. Satan would have loved for me to fall away from God altogether—praise God that by His grace, I didn't. One thing that turned my life—emotions, body, and spirit—around was a simple question from my Christian counselor: "Why do you think God is not big or powerful enough to handle your pain?"

As I wrestled with that question and its answers, another friend— herself a trained counselor—gave me another aha moment. She said, "Dena, if we had perfect parents, we wouldn't need God."

Just as Nabal's abuse caused Abigail to become strong in the Lord, my experience with an imperfect father caused me to be drawn to my heavenly Father. If my father had been the kind of dad I wanted, I probably wouldn't have felt the need for God that I did as a child and a teenager. And I probably wouldn't have been as motivated to leave home and find adventure. In fact, God called me to ministry at the age of eleven, and He's allowed me to serve Him in all sorts of jobs—missionary, author, mom, wife, speaker, entertainer, teacher—all over the world and in forty-six states.

I like this advice from Howard E. Butt Jr.:

> I'm not saying we need to get it out in the open in a knock-down-drag-out fight with those we feel have betrayed us. Sometimes a wise openness with them may be necessary, but often—even usually—it's not. What *is* necessary is for us to get fully in touch with our anger, to confess before God our bitterness, to claim His crucifixion-resurrection triumph in it all, and to give thanks ahead of time for His victory in us, including our ability to love the person we feel has sinned against us so grievously.[1]

You may not believe it right now, but God (and only God) has the power not only to help you forgive your abuser, but also to love them. It takes time, godly guidance, and His healing presence, but miracles are His specialty. And as my pastor, Mark Forrest, says, "The greatest miracle is a changed life." Victory can be yours—if you truly desire it.

When we are in an abusive relationship, we often determine, "God must not love me anymore" or "I'm not loveable." (Tina says, "The truth is, we women in abusive relationships often stop loving ourselves—making it more likely that we'll remain in the abuse.")

Have you said similar words to yourself? Dear sister, I pray you will learn the truth. You are so loveable that God sent His only Son to ransom you! He created you as His precious daughter. You have immense

---

1. Howard E. Butt Jr., *Who Can You Trust? Overcoming Betrayal and Fear* (Colorado Springs: WaterBrook, 2004), 48.

value and worth. Replace the names *Israel* and *Jacob* in this passage with
your own, and read Isaiah 43:1–4 to yourself:

> But now, this is what the LORD says—
>   he who created you, Jacob,
>   he who formed you, Israel:
> "Do not fear, for I have redeemed you;
>   I have summoned you by name; you are mine.
> When you pass through the waters,
>   I will be with you;
> and when you pass through the rivers,
>   they will not sweep over you.
> When you walk through the fire,
>   you will not be burned;
>   the flames will not set you ablaze.
> For I am the LORD your God,
>   the Holy One of Israel, your Savior;
> I give Egypt for your ransom,
>   Cush and Seba in your stead.
> Since you are precious and honored in my sight,
>   and because I love you."

TINA ❧ Once we've determined to see ourselves as God sees us,
we begin to love ourselves as He loves us. Then we'll understand what
is OK in our relationships and what is *not* OK. Only then will we be
ready to make changes.

Randy Alcorn wrote from his book, *The Goodness of God*:

> Many people start to doubt God's care when terrible things
> happen to them. Often it's because we define love in superficial

and trivial ways, setting us up to question God in hard times. But the Bible speaks repeatedly of God's *unfailing* or *steadfast* love (as in Psalms 32:10 and 51:1, and Lamentations 3:32, NIV and ESV). God's constant love for us will never let us down, no matter how things appear. When we define God's love as we please, then use that redefinition to neutralize other attributes of God that we find less appealing, we mirror our culture which values love and devalues holiness. Elevating God's love above his other character traits can breed resentment, anger, confusion, and disappointment when he allows us to suffer.[2]

What wisdom! We all have preconceived notions about how God should express His love and care for us. When God doesn't meet our expectations, our view of Him changes. That view—if it is unhealthy—can cause us to carry "resentment, anger, confusion, and disappointment" toward God.

If we also dismiss the fact that God can use and work in all things, we are minimizing God's wisdom. Such a place makes it difficult to evaluate our wounds and to put them into perspective.

The Healing Process

Beloved one, you can take steps in forgiving those who have hurt you. Each step you take toward healing your own heart will bring you closer to God, and closer to forgiving the one who hurt you.

God wants the deepest part of the wound. The deepest part of you. The deepest part of the hurt.

When you have worked your way to the deepest part (with God's abundant love), you will find freedom. When you understand your value and worth, you will find freedom. When you fully love yourself

---

2. Randy Alcorn, *The Goodness of God: Assurance of God in the Midst of Suffering* (Portland, OR: Multnomah, 2010), 33.

and love God, you will find freedom. Forgiveness will come through God's love, and you will have the freedom you so desperately desire.

Someday, you will also be able to minister to others who've gone through abuse. Pastor Mark says, "God's miracles aren't done just to reduce pain—but to reveal who Jesus is." Once we've seen Jesus and He has ministered to us, we can't help but point others to Him. We want them to experience His healing power too!

In the meantime, start working on *you*. Get into a recovery program. Join a Bible study. Pray for yourself; pray for—when you're able to—your abuser. Meditate on God's Word and place Scripture cards where you will continually see them—in your car, bathroom, kitchen, office cubicle, and so on. Find a Christian counselor and begin peeling away the layers.

Taking steps toward healing can make you feel very fearful and vulnerable, so remember to drench yourself in Jesus's living water. God will be the soothing balm for your wounds.

We can count on it.

3

Dinah

From Vulnerable to Victim

❧ Genesis 34 ❧

Tina ❧ *I hope this is the right path, God.* My mind swirled as we pulled into our new, small Colorado town. Before unpacking, we headed to the main strip and drove from one end of town to the other, soaking up every detail. Our children were young, and I can remember pointing out the schools, park, and McDonald's. In a sense, we were all like children, needing to be familiar with every element of our new city.

Deep inside, I wondered what would unfold—if I would find much-needed friends, whether my kids would be happy in the schools, and how my husband would like his new job. Our journeys to new places don't always end the way we envision. Sometimes our experiences exceed our expectations, while at other times the hardships seem to outweigh the good.

Unspeakable Violation

Dinah's family had just arrived in the land of Canaan. Her father, Jacob, purchased a piece of ground near the city of Shechem. It was a beautiful place, nestled in a valley between Mt. Gerizim and Mt. Ebal. After pitching his tent, Jacob immediately set up an altar and called it El Elohe Israel—"the mighty God of Israel." Jacob had a love for God—and a heart full of praise.

Imagine Dinah as a vibrant young woman, curious and longing to experience the world. She would have been a teenager, but she had probably reached the age where she could soon marry. Though the altar and valley where they had settled seemed important to her father, Dinah longed to explore a new and unfamiliar place.

After the move, Dinah "went out to visit the women of the land" (Gen. 34:1).

I love that about Dinah. She didn't say she wanted to shop at the market or catch the city sights; she longed to visit the women of the land. Dinah had been raised with six brothers and six half brothers. Since she was the only girl in the family, I'm sure her brothers were protective of her. But it also makes sense that Dinah longed to connect with other women her age.

Dinah strolled through the countryside and soaked up every beautiful detail. I imagine her bouncing through the fields and picking wildflowers as she headed into the city. Or maybe she strolled down a dusty road and kicked at the stones. Either way, I'm sure she made her way into the city with anticipation and excitement.

He stood in the distance and as she entered the city, his eyes followed. Twisting through the crowd, he made his way to her. Did a fresh new face fascinate him, or was the beauty of Dinah so captivating that it glistened? It drew him to her. He followed her with a great intensity.

Each city in that day was governed individually, so Shechem would have been considered a prince, because he was the son of Hamor the Hivite, the ruler of the city. At first glance, one might believe that this young man was quite a catch. He was held in high esteem among the people. His standing as the son of the ruler of the city was enough to fascinate any woman.

What thoughts crowded Shechem's mind as he watched Dinah? At some point, a spirit of lust rose up within him so strongly that he acted upon his licentious passion. Shechem raped Dinah, daughter of Jacob (v. 2). Though the Bible doesn't say exactly how it happened, many translations use the word *rape*. Some scholars believe that Dinah wasn't really raped, but was taken advantage of. Whatever version of Scripture we choose to use, however, the words speak for themselves: "violated" (NKJV), "humiliated" (ESV), and "lay with her by force" (NASB).

Not much detail is given to what unfolded, but we can visualize that horrific scene. I imagine Dinah felt utterly helpless and defiled. Did she sit weeping afterward? Let us envision that, at the sight of her tears, Shechem's tone began to change. Suddenly, "his heart was drawn to Dinah daughter of Jacob; he loved the young woman and spoke tenderly to her. And Shechem said to his father Hamor, 'Get me this girl as my wife'" (vv. 3–4).

We understand that it wasn't true love that Shechem experienced, because true love doesn't express itself in this manner. Filled with infatuation, passion, and obsession (like a spoiled child), Shechem announced to his father, as he had no doubt done numerous times before, "Get me this." In that moment, Dinah, like so many other women, had become an object and a convenience.

Now picture the aching heart of such an innocent young woman. Her wounded body, spirit, and soul lay trembling in the place where he "took her." Those of you who have been wounded in this vile manner can identify with Dinah. In fact, at this very moment, emotions may be flooding your heart.

It doesn't take much to trigger a wound. Just reading about someone else's victimization can take us back to a place we haven't visited in a very long time. To use an onion analogy, we have now peeled back a layer—and it stings. However, the only way to find healing for our wound is to pull back what's been concealing it, and allow God to cover the pain with His healing strength.

When I was a little girl, I was sexually violated. I really didn't understand the impact of the act until I grew old enough to process through what had happened. I suppressed my feelings for so long that I actually lived without that memory, except through dreams. I remember having a few dreams about being sexually abused, but I thought they were just nightmares. It wasn't until I went to college and underwent training at the Carl Perkins Center for the Prevention of Child Abuse that the wound was exposed.

The training was pretty intense, and on the very last day, we watched a video of two young teens confronting the one who sexually assaulted them. As I watched, emotions boiled within me. I wrestled with an ache I could not identify. Suddenly, memories came flooding back, as if someone were rewinding a videotape. It was a strange sensation. In that moment, I realized that the so-called nightmares were not nightmares at all. They were real!

Tears streamed down my cheeks. I jumped up and ran out of the room, out of the building. My chest heaving, panic-stricken, I doubled over to catch my breath. Realizing I had been violated was an unbearable blow. A counselor had seen my distress and followed me. I paced and walked while the wonderful counselor tried to keep up. For a long while, I couldn't even speak. Where was I? I felt like I was in someone else's life, someone else's body. I wanted to shout, "No—this didn't happen to me!"

Now I can see the reason I was asked to go to the training at that particular time in my life. It was as if God was saying, "Okay, Tina . . . today is the day I strip away the Band-Aid. And it's really going to hurt for a while. But I promise I will never leave your side, and though you can't see it right now, this is a good thing. Only I can heal the wound that has been festering."

Lashing Out

When Jacob heard that his daughter Dinah had been defiled, his sons were in the fields with his livestock; so he did nothing about it until they came home.

> Then Shechem's father Hamor went out to talk with Jacob. Meanwhile, Jacob's sons had come in from the fields as soon as they heard what had happened. They were shocked and furious, because Shechem had done an outrageous thing in Israel by sleeping with Jacob's daughter—a thing that should not be done. (Gen. 34:5–7)

The men in Dinah's life reacted in different ways. Her brothers were angry, hurt, and—rightly so—felt violated themselves. When someone we love is abused, we often find ourselves wanting to lash out.

Jacob was silent, which some might interpret as weakness. However, his heart was close to God, and though he did not outwardly speak, the Lord understood the anguish in his heart. Sometimes it takes more strength to sit silently with the Lord than to charge forward into the chaos.

> But Hamor said to them, "My son Shechem has his heart set on your daughter. Please give her to him as his wife. Intermarry with us; give us your daughters and take our daughters for yourselves. You can settle among us; the land is open to you. Live in it, trade in it, and acquire property in it." (vv. 8–10)

The request for Dinah had been made. After everyone negotiated and bargained, the brothers came up with a scheme: take revenge on those who had orchestrated their sister's painful circumstances.

Dinah's siblings told Shechem that every man in the city would need to be circumcised before any of them could intermarry. Hamor and Shechem agreed, and hurriedly had all of the men in the city circumcised. The fact that all of the men in the city would submit to such an act shows the respect they had for their ruler.

And in the midst of the men's weakness, pain, and vulnerability, Simeon and Levi took their swords and murdered every man in the city. The brothers were so full of rage that they killed innocent men who had nothing to do with the rape of their sister. Not only did they kill the men, but afterward, the rest of the brothers helped loot the city. They took everything of value, including the women and children! The brothers also put a sword to Hamor and Shechem and delivered Dinah back to their family home.

Can we imagine having that much anger over a wound we suffered? Of course we can. It's perfectly normal to feel angry, betrayed, and confused about any kind of sexual violation. But what we do with our pain matters.

As I read through this passage, I kept asking myself, What happened to Dinah? How did *she* cope? What did *she* do? How did she live out the rest of her days? The biblical account ends there, but her story went on. Similarly, victims in today's world often fade away as well. Due to shame, guilt, and fear—and others' ignorance—their voices often go unheard in the midst of life's cacophony.

It doesn't have to work that way, however. As for me, I never wanted to lash back at my abusers, but I did have to work through my anger, sadness, and grief. It was incredibly painful. After all, stripping away layers of protection to get to the heart of a wound isn't easy. But going through the pain was worth it, because I ultimately found freedom.

I started getting counseling, worked through my pain, and tried to understand what had happened. That required asking tough questions, sharing my wound with those closest to me, and empathizing with the perpetrator (yes, even that). It meant coming to a realization that as a young child, I was the one violated. I had done nothing wrong. I also began to understand that I didn't want to carry the perpetrator's shame. I could let it go. Most importantly, I kept walking with the Lord.

From Darkness to Light

When we have been wounded, there are two ways to run: toward God or away from Him. We get to choose. Running away from God and trying to deal with something like abuse on our own is extremely risky. There are no guarantees that we'll have the strength to do it alone; more than likely, we will not.

Running away from God means that we may find ourselves lashing out—seeking our own revenge—and retaliating in some way. When we lash back, the victim becomes the perpetrator. Sadly, it's a common tale. Running away from our heavenly Father also means that we begin to harbor bitterness, hurt, anger, and unforgiveness, rather than handing such a heavy load over to God and allowing Him to carry it for us.

But how do we run toward a God who we feel didn't protect us? Do we say to ourselves, as the psalmist did, "My bones suffer mortal agony as my foes taunt me, saying to me all day long, 'Where is your God?'" (Ps. 42:10).

The world can be a very dark place, and when we're faced with sexual violation of any kind, it's hard to comprehend. Though God gives each of us choices and the opportunity to do the right thing, there are those who choose disobedience. The result of disobedience to God is always pain and wounds. We wound ourselves, and we wound others. Your abuser disobeyed God, and you were wounded. But God sees.

He sees!

"But you, God, see the trouble of the afflicted; you consider their grief and take it in hand. The victims commit themselves to you; you are the helper of the fatherless" (Ps. 10:14). The psalmist was saying God sees all things and if we commit, release, and surrender ourselves, as well as our wounds, to God, He will bring healing to our lives.

Job suffered greatly without understanding why. Though his friends tried to convince him it was due to his sin, he chose not to surrender to such talk. Instead, he chose to believe that God had a reason for whatever He was allowing to happen. Job said to his friends, "Where then does wisdom come from? Where does understanding dwell? It is hidden from the eyes of every living thing, concealed even from the birds in the sky. Destruction and Death say, 'Only a rumor of it has reached our ears.' God understands the way to it and he alone knows where it dwells, for he views the ends of the earth and sees everything under the heavens" (Job 28:20–24). Job understood one important fact: God sees. Yes, truly, the God who made the heavens and earth, who commands the mornings, sends forth the lightning, hangs the clouds, and who created something far more precious than earth, who created *us*—does see all things. And though we may not understand our wounding, God does.

I'll never forget the year my family and I visited a cave. Our tour guide took us deep beneath the surface of the ground. At our first stop, she began explaining the depth of the cave and how it had been formed. Then she asked us to turn our lights off. The darkness suffocated me. I felt as if I might hyperventilate. I couldn't wait for her to say, "You can now turn your lights back on."

As I reflect back on that moment, I realize that wounds can feel a lot like that dark cave. But the Lord also reminds me of one thing: I held the flashlight in my hand. I could have turned it on anytime I wanted.

Just as Jesus asked the man who had been an invalid for thirty-eight years, He asks us, "Do you want to get well?" (John 5:6). There are days when we feel as if we can't take two steps forward, much less make it down the road.

But if we want to get well, we do take small steps—one at a time. Second Corinthians 5:7 says we walk by faith and not by sight. In faith we understand that God will never, ever leave us (Heb. 13:5) and that no one can snatch us out of His hand (John 10:28). With Him holding our hand, we have the grace to move out of our pain and into the light. Eventually, we find that we're making progress.

And as we walk with Him, we begin to see that God *Himself* is the light that leads us through the darkness. We don't have to live in the dark; we can grab hold of the light: "This is the message we have heard from him and declare to you: God is light; in him there is no darkness at all" (1 John 1:5).

She wants me to face my wound? you may be asking yourself. *I could never do that.* I told myself that very thing once. It was scary; the thought of facing what I'd endured made me nauseous. At the beginning of my healing journey, I cried a lot. But over time, I could actually speak to someone about my abuse without crying. It was as if God had pulled back the curtains of a dark room and I was peeking out at a bright blue sky. What a glorious place!

Years later, the Lord placed on my heart that I needed to tell one of the persons who abused me that I forgave him. I knew he wasn't the same person anymore; at the time of the abuse, he was just a kid. I had already forgiven him, but he needed to hear it. One day, at just the right time, the Lord opened the door for me to visit with him.

After saying, "I forgive you," I watched as his strong shoulders shuddered and tears fell to the floor. Then he said, "I have really been longing to hear that." At that moment, my freedom became his.

My dear sister, your freedom awaits. Step into the light.

DENA 🌸 I've never suffered sexual abuse, but I know many, many women who have. There was at least one relationship in my teenage years that came close to abuse. When I was a senior in high school, a coach flirted shamelessly with me during a daily P.E. class. I was flattered by the attention, instead of being repulsed. As a "brainy," nice girl who didn't date much in high school, an older man's attentions gave me a boost of confidence. This man wasn't even that attractive, but he made me feel beautiful. (Back then, sexual harassment wasn't something we were taught to watch out for.)

Because the coach and I were never alone, no abuse occurred. However, he was often seen around town with one of my classmates, and in my freshman year of college, I heard that he had been fired because my classmate had finally admitted their relationship was sexual.

If you're one of those who has been victimized (most likely by a person you trusted), my heart breaks for you. I wish I could sit with you and listen to your story, give you a hug, and cry with you.

One survivor answered honestly when I asked her if God had healed her, "Has God healed my wounds? If healing means there's no more pain, no after-effects, then no, He hasn't. There are movies I can't watch, relationships I can't pursue. I still deal with panic attacks, flashbacks, dreams. But God graciously shows me His work in others and in me, turning the damage to good. I think that's healing."

He's Enough

My friend Megan sat with a spiritual director during her college years, and in several sessions, the director told her about God's abilities to heal memories. In spite of the director's advice, Megan resisted asking God where He was, specifically, during some of her most painful circumstances.

Megan says, "When I was about eighteen months old, I suffered some kind of severe physical abuse while under the care of my grandparents. That's vague, but it's all I can tell you definitively. God has graciously revealed scenes—as if a camera in a fixed place was recording—as I listen to other people's stories. The facts are these: I was black and blue from head to toe, and I was admitted to the hospital with a 108 degree fever."

A couple of years ago, Megan stopped resisting. She bravely asked God, "Where were you? I mean literally. Show me where you were in this awful situation."

He spoke to her spirit: *I was the fever.*

Megan was stunned when she heard God's pronouncement; she would have never imagined that particular answer. But then she realized that the fever was His gift to her: "My grandmother would never have taken me to the ER without it. She would have been too afraid of people finding out the truth. But with a fever that high, she had no choice. It was life or death. I really think God sent the fever so that I could get medical attention."

Megan's abusers continued hurting her, with the abuse growing increasingly sexual. "I also lost hearing in one ear due to the high fever and further trauma," she says. "By the time I was seven, I was having nightmares every night. I told God, 'If you don't give me a good dream, I will never go to sleep again.' And He gave me a dream of heaven. Jesus came into my room and escorted me up the golden ladder. I saw my dogs that had been run over, my real grandfather who died before I was born, and God Himself, on a carved wooden throne. He showed me the books of life, including the one with my name on it. We looked at my book, and He helped explain things to me."

Through her dreams and the spiritual direction, Megan began to realize that God was there, even in her darkest moments—that He cared. She says, "The abuse did eventually stop. My step-grandfather died in a Nabal-like fashion."

God sustained Megan through the next few years, when both her parents got cancer and other family trauma occurred. She explains, "When my mom told me that if I asked Jesus into my heart, He would never leave, I roller-skated down the driveway and knelt on the steps in the garage and prayed. He came."

She says, "I could go on and on with sad things, some occurring right now. But at age forty, God is still revealing Himself to me. I find comfort knowing that Christ knows what it is to suffer and not be delivered. He took my sickness upon Himself. That's enough."

My pastor, who lived through trauma I can't imagine during his childhood, says that you'll never know God is all you need until God is all you have.

I can attest to that. So can Megan, who found that God's presence was enough to sustain her during incredibly painful circumstances. So can Stephanie, another survivor of sexual abuse I met when we worked in the same building. She served as a counselor for homeless families in our school district, and I worked as a communications director for a nonprofit. We bonded over our love for Jesus—and our passion for writing out our own experiences in order to encourage others. Because she is a survivor, a counselor, and an excellent writer, I asked her to share her journey and some advice for those who need healing. She graciously agreed.

Stephanie's Story

Like any woman, Dinah desired to be desired, and yet her heart was crushed.

After suffering my own abuse, I laid on my bedroom floor. I begged for intervention . . . hope . . . something to pull me out of this emotional turmoil I laid buried in. "God, help me," I cried out. "Don't You know what has happened to me?"

Silence. My Father was silent. My heart refused to listen to the reasoning that silence could be beneficial. I wanted a rescue. I needed a rescue. I cried myself to sleep.

Following Dinah's rape, her father remained silent as well. Can you imagine how this broke her heart? No anger, no outrage—just silence. The word used for "silent" in this passage can also be translated "held his peace." Dinah's father "held his peace." Could it be that my Father was holding His peace, holding my peace?

Peace is not a word I would use to describe my battles. It was a struggle to keep my head above water, to make it through every day without having a complete emotional breakdown. I cried out to God day and night, and yet I felt so utterly and completely alone. He was silent.

He knew there was not an answer to my questions that would satisfy me. He knew I needed to feel my emotions. He knew I was hurting. He knew it was hard, but He never, ever stopped keeping the peace.

And when the time came, I reached up, stopped asking questions, and grasped the hand of the One who holds the peace.

People often ask me how I healed. Healing from sexual assault is not easy. I've seen that in my own healing, as well as in my work as a professional counselor-intern. I've heard from women who've endured such physical abuse that they weren't even able to have children. This kind of trauma leaves deep emotional scars.

I wish I could provide some kind of formula for healing—that if you followed certain steps, all your pain would go away. That's simply not possible, but what I *can* offer you is what I have seen work for myself and others:

1. *Seek wise, Christian, professional counsel.* Professional counselors are trained to work with trauma. Going to a counselor might seem scary at first, perhaps because you've previously had a bad experience with a counselor. Let me encourage you to seek the *right* person. A very important element of counseling is the therapeutic relationship, so choose a counselor who "gets you" and whom you can trust implicitly. [*Note from Dena*: If you don't think you have the money to pay for professional help, check with your health plan. Most of them now have some kind of coverage for mental health issues. Also, many churches have funds to help their members pay for such services—no questions asked. And counselors often work on a sliding scale, taking income into consideration when charging fees.]

2. *Find a support group.* There's great value in being surrounded by other women who have experienced the same circumstances. However, when choosing a support group, be cautious. You want to choose a group where the focus is on healing. If the "vibe" of the group seems negative, it might not be the right group for you.

3. *Don't rule out medication.* Antidepressants and antianxiety medications can be a part of the healing process. If the levels of serotonin and other neurotransmitters are depleted in your brain, medication can return these levels to normal. Medication is not for everyone, but it can

be effective in treating the symptoms often experienced by survivors of sexual assault.

4. Join a Bible study. I encourage you to spend time in God's Word every day, not just in solitude, but also in group study. If face-to-face group study seems too intimidating at first, you may want to try an online Bible study. The value of studying God's Word in a group is that you become surrounded by sisters who will speak truth and positive affirmation into your life. We often have plenty of negative voices in our lives. Bible study refills us with God's truth.

5. Memorize Scripture. Have you ever stopped to notice the damaging scripts that run through your head? Satan likes to plant thoughts in our minds, such as: "I'm not good enough" or "I deserved it" or "I'm dirty." Those are all lies that need to be countered with Scripture. You may have told yourself these lies for years, so don't expect them to disappear overnight. However, if you make a conscious and concerted effort to replace these lies with scriptural truth, you'll undergo a transformation of the mind. [*Note from Dena*: When I was going through severe depression, I put index cards with Bible verses all over the house, in my car, and at work. That way, any time I noticed a negative thought creeping into my brain, I was immediately able to review God's truth and replace the lies with His Word. Over time, God healed me from dysfunctional thinking and I found freedom. His Word is a living, powerful thing!]

6. Cry out. Don't be afraid to get vocal with God. One of my favorite Scriptures comes from Mark 9:24: "Immediately the boy's father exclaimed, 'I do believe; help me overcome my unbelief!'" At times, we refuse to seek God and the healing He offers, simply because we believe the wrong things. We believe we are shamed, broken, and not worth anything—instead of believing in God's amazing truth. The truth is that He loves you, you are His princess, and you are chosen and beautiful in His eyes. Dear sister, He will re-gift you with anything you feel was taken from you. Cry out to Him, over and over again, "Help me overcome my unbelief."

7. Have hope. Hope can be translated as "confident expectation." Expect God's healing. Don't fix your eyes on your circumstances, because circumstances change. God, however, is unchanging. Fix your eyes on Him—and only Him. He is the One who can provide full and pervasive healing to your wounds. As His Word says in Isaiah 61:1–3,

> The Spirit of the Sovereign Lord is on me, because the Lord has anointed me to proclaim good news to the poor. He has sent me to bind up the brokenhearted, to proclaim freedom for the captives and release from darkness for the prisoners, to proclaim the year of the Lord's favor and the day of vengeance of our God, to comfort all who mourn, and provide for those who grieve in Zion—to bestow on them a crown of beauty instead of ashes, the oil of joy instead of mourning, and a garment of praise instead of a spirit of despair. They will be called oaks of righteousness, a planting of the Lord for the display of his splendor.

Stephanie is a wounded warrior who shares the healing power of Jesus with every person she meets. I can testify to her healing, because before I ever officially met her, I had the sense that she was a sister in Christ. She absolutely glowed with His love.

I'll forever be grateful to God, who in His perfect providence arranged for us to work in the same building at the same time.

When Stephanie and I first met, I worked at a charity that resettled refugees from all over the world. In cooperation with the US State

Department and national resettlement services, our agency helped these victims of war and persecution to start over in the United States. We provided them with a furnished apartment, pocket money, English classes, transportation, and job training. Our case managers enrolled the children in school and helped the parents get immunized and acculturated to a brand-new place, far from the home they were forced to leave.

As I began to hear the refugees' stories through our trained interpreters, I realized that many of them had been raped and tortured by their fellow human beings. It was hard for me to fathom.

One day, a coworker came into my cubicle, her face cloudy. Beside her stood a Burmese girl who'd recently arrived from another city. The child's black pageboy framed a heart-shaped face with dark eyes.

"Hi, sweetie," I said, even though I knew she couldn't understand a word of English.

My coworker told me about the girl's family: Her sister had been raped in a refugee camp at the age of twelve. She had become pregnant, and had delivered the baby after arriving in America. The teen, her baby, her father, and the child in front of me had come on their own to our city, so they weren't connected to a resettlement agency and lacked access to any kind of assistance. They'd survived unthinkable crimes and a journey across the planet—and now, they were just barely scratching out an existence.

"All they have in their apartment is a dirty mattress," said my coworker. "We're going to give them some clothes and a few other things."

As the child's father met with a caseworker, I gave my new friend a children's book. She edged toward me a tiny bit as she saw the colorful illustrations. I smiled and showed her how to open the pop-up flaps. "See? There are hidden pictures."

"You can have it," I said, longing to take her on my lap, stroke her hair. Clutching the gift, she ran off. I followed. As I did, I noticed her clothes were dirty and her shoes were at least two sizes too big. They barely stayed on her small brown feet.

Suddenly, a wave of sorrow crashed over me. The truth about the things she and her family had experienced—along with the other stories I'd heard since starting this job—threatened to drown me. Angry, I sucked in my breath.

Where are you, God? I thought.

Where.

Are.

You?

And then, as audibly as if He'd spoken it aloud to me, I heard: "I'm in *you.*"

The truth of it gave me my breath back.

Yes, I thought.

Yes.

I nodded, sighed, and caught up to my new friend. Gently, I took her hand.

She smiled up at me, and didn't let go.

4

Ruth

From Grief to Gratitude

✢ THE BOOK OF RUTH ✢

TINA ✢ During a time in the Old Testament when judges ruled the land, a great famine broke out in Judah. While some people stayed in the Promised Land, others scattered to places where they could feed their families.

Elimelek stood behind Naomi and watched her forcefully scrub at the linens. "In two days we leave for Moab," he said.

Naomi jerked her head around, "Elimelek!" She stood to her feet and her eyes reached his. Her face softened as she placed her hand to her heart. "This is our home. Must we leave so soon? Surely the rains will come. The God of Abraham—"

"Rains! What rains?" Elimelek threw his arms in the air and paced forward. "If we do not want to starve our sons or ourselves to death, then we must leave. There is no food. The ground is too dry to plant. The rains haven't fallen in quite some time and what little food the townspeople had is now plundered. No. We must!" Elimelek placed his hand upon Naomi's shoulder and she gently laid her head against his warm body. A distressed feeling ran through her and she whispered, "But why Moab?"

In order to save his family from potential ruin, Elimelek took them from Bethlehem and moved to Moab. No one knows how the real story of that decision unfolded, and some scholars believe that Elimelek left in haste, with his impatience getting the best of him. Who knows what we would do in similar circumstances? We've all been there.

When I was a little girl I couldn't understand why we had to move so many times. My father had his reasons for moving; there were times when the need to survive took over. Sometimes we lived in parks, tents, or old houses. Wherever we laid our heads—sometimes it was on the floorboard of a car—my father always found a way to feed us. Though there were times when the food was scarce, we never went without. As I grew older and began to work through my resentment of having to move so much, I realized that my father did what he knew how to do. Though the paths he chose were not always good, I saw that he always labored to care for and feed his family.

Some people believe that the move to Moab proved disastrous for Elimelek and his family (and perhaps it did). However, what looks detrimental to us, God, in His mercy, can make beneficial.

Israel and Moab had a long history of conflict, and the Lord gave countless instructions to the Israelites regarding the country of Moab and the people who lived there. In addition, the God of Israel often forbade the Israelites to enter the land or to intermarry with the Moabites. However, the Israelite men were often enamored with the Moabite women and ignored God's commands, engaging in sexual immorality and idol worship: "While Israel was staying in Shittim, the men began to indulge in sexual immorality with Moabite women, who invited them to the sacrifices to their gods. The people ate the sacrificial meal and bowed down before these gods. So Israel yoked themselves to the Baal of Peor. And the LORD's anger burned against them" (Num. 25:1–3).

In Numbers 22, when the Israelites were approaching the Promised

Land, the Moabites enlisted Balaam to curse them. But God loved His people enough that He would not allow Balaam to curse them, only to bless them.

In Judges, God gave the king of Moab power over Israel (Judg. 3:12) for eighteen years before he delivered them from Moab. The Moabites worshipped the god of Chemosh, and practiced human sacrifice, which included children—something the Lord spoke against. I find it interesting that out of all the places Elimelek could have taken his family, he chose to move to Moab. Again we ask, why Moab?

Sadly, at some point during their stay in Moab, Elimelek died. We don't know how he died or how long he lived in Moab before his death. While the family resided in Moab, Naomi's sons, Mahlon and Kilion, came of age and married women outside of their religion—Orpah and Ruth. Ruth, whose famous words of commitment to Naomi are spoken in many wedding ceremonies, was a Moabite woman.

> Now Elimelek, Naomi's husband, died, and she was left with her two sons. They married Moabite women, one named Orpah and the other Ruth. After they had lived there about ten years, both Mahlon and Kilion also died, and Naomi was left without her two sons and her husband. (Ruth 1:3–5)

Ruth's Wound

No one knows how long Ruth was married to her husband before he died, but the Scriptures make it clear that they didn't have children. So many questions run through our minds as we read her story: How long were they married? How did her husband die? What was her marriage like? What we do know is that the wound of losing someone we love can be one of the most difficult wounds to endure.

As a music therapist, part of my training required that I become educated as a facilitator for the American Cancer Society. Over the years, I have been able to facilitate grief support groups, as well as teach on recovering from losses in life. I'll never forget one widow I met in one of the groups. She was a beautiful woman in her late fifties. I asked what brought her to the meeting, and she responded, "I can't seem to get over the loss of my husband."

"How long has it been since he died?" I asked.

Her response? "Twenty-five years."

I was shocked. She had been grieving for a quarter of a century— which meant that her husband died while she was in her twenties. My heart sank. She had never remarried or moved on. She found herself camped out at one of the stages of grief, unable to move past it. It had literally stolen much of her life.

Though I've never lost a spouse, I have endured grief in many shapes and forms. And I know from personal experience and from my work as a therapist that we can either embrace our losses and work through them, or store them somewhere deep within us. Trust me: those stored emotions will find a way to surface.

It was October 7, 2001. Almost one month after the 9/11 attack on the United States, America launched their war with Afghanistan. That Sunday not only changed our entire world, but it also changed my family in a way I never dreamed possible.

I arrived home from church that day, checked my voice messages, and heard that one of my brothers wanted me to call him back right away. I'll never forget his words: "There was a shooting at the VA hospital."

As the world watched our troops battle from afar, another war occurred in a small Texas town. One of the residents at the veterans' hospital, known for having psychotic episodes, stalked three men who were also undergoing medical treatment. He had no idea who they were, and none of the three patients knew each other. Due to the man's mental state of mind, he actually thought that all three were somehow connected with the Mafia.

Over time, the man planned his attack. And on October 7, 2001, he waited in the cafeteria for the first one to enter. After the first man sat down with his plate of food, the gunman walked up to him, placed the pistol to his victim's temple, and pulled the trigger. The innocent man was killed instantly.

That man was my brother.

I'll never forget the moment I found out about his murder. After more than ten years, the wound still hurts. So although I don't know how it feels to lose a husband—whether through death or divorce—I've definitely felt the sting of losing someone I truly love.

No one's journey through grief will look the same, and everyone will grieve in different ways. After hearing the news about my brother, all I could do was sit at the piano in a state of numbness and play. For three days, I couldn't speak.

I sat with my eyes closed, and allowed my fingers to move up and down the piano. The melodies resonated throughout the room and found a place in the center of the darkness. My heart seeped with profound pain. My soul felt empty and lost; yet in the stillness, music came forth and filled the room. Somehow, in my moments of despair, God's Spirit settled on me and my tears flowed freely.

In the midst of my grief, music became the words I could not speak. Embracing the wound was the only way I could get through it.

A Matter of Choice

After the death of her husband and sons, Naomi was faced with decisions that would affect her life, and the lives of her daughters-in-law, Ruth and Orpah.

> When Naomi heard in Moab that the LORD had come to the aid of his people by providing food for them, she and her daughters-in-law prepared to return home from there. With her two daughters-in-law she left the place where she had been living and set out on the road that would take them back to the land of Judah. (Ruth 1:6–7)

At some point, Naomi turned to her daughters-in-law and told them to go back to their homes: "At this they wept aloud again. Then Orpah kissed her mother-in-law goodbye, but Ruth clung to her. 'Look,' said Naomi, 'your sister-in-law is going back to her people and her gods. Go back with her'" (vv. 14–15).

Suddenly, something unexpected happened. Ruth, with her wounded heart, decided to make a change. At that very moment, she chose to leave the place of loss and move forward with her mother-in-law, Naomi.

> "Don't urge me to leave you or to turn back from you. Where you go I will go, and where you stay I will stay. Your people will be my people and your God my God. Where you die I will die, and there I will be buried. May the LORD deal with me, be it ever so severely, if even death separates you and me." When Naomi realized that Ruth was determined to go with her, she stopped urging her. (vv. 16–18)

Ruth turned from her land, her family, and most importantly, from the idols she grew up worshipping—and boldly declared that Naomi's God would now become hers. It's amazing, really. After all, Ruth could have gone back to her old ways. She could have gone back and married a man from her country, and she could have gone back to her family.

As I studied this text, my eyes were opened to a new thought: suppose this was Ruth's way of following not only this Israelite family, but also God. Is it possible that Ruth's profound declaration had more to do with God than Naomi?

It was no small feat for Ruth to venture away from all she'd ever known, especially as a widowed woman. But oh, what an awesome God we serve! He used the seal of Ruth's wedding vows into Naomi's family to change Ruth. How fitting that we use her words to complement our wedding vows today! I have often heard my husband say to couples,

"Perhaps God gave you your spouse not for you to change them, but so that God can use the relationship to change you."

It reminds me of the famous words from another biblical heroine's story. Could it be that Ruth was placed in her husband's family just like Esther was placed in the king's palace, "for such a time as this" (Esther 4:14)? Is it too difficult to imagine that something good could come from such a wound? That even in the midst of our wounds God can do exactly as He promised—continue a good work in us and carry it on to completion (Phil. 1:6)? Of course He can.

Regardless, Ruth had to be willing to make a change. And her new journey was not going to be easy. Women in Old Testament times were often looked down upon and thought to be inferior to men.

Ruth choosing to leave her old life and step into a new one, didn't mean she wouldn't face obstacles or fear. The journey ahead would include finding work, food, a place to live, friendships, and people who would accept a single Moabite woman in an Israelite community—a land God promised the Israelites. It meant trying to survive as a woman during a time men were considered to be of greater value.[1] It meant facing the shame of not having a husband, land, or inheritance.

When we've lost someone close to us and choose to move forward, there is fear in the unknown. We get to choose to run toward something healthy or unhealthy. There are roadblocks to hurdle, challenges to conquer, and painful emotions to sort through. But God, in His tenderness, waits for us. He tries to settle our hearts and when we are ready, He steps with us. That is something I admire about Ruth—she choose to *move*. Though stepping back into her old life would likely have meant safety and security with her family, it would have also meant

---

1. See Leviticus 27:1–4, for instance: "The LORD said to Moses, 'Speak to the Israelites and say to them: 'If anyone makes a special vow to dedicate a person to the LORD by giving the equivalent value, set the value of a male between the ages of twenty and sixty at fifty shekels of silver, according to the sanctuary shekel; for a female, set her value at thirty shekels.'"

going back to her culture and the gods they worshipped. Ruth stepped toward something she had learned from the family she married into—a life of an Israelite and the God they served. She chose the better path.

From Moab to a Miracle

Ruth and Naomi eventually found their way back to Bethlehem. As Naomi declared her bitterness to the other women in town, Ruth lived as a foreigner, having to fear exploitation. She faced vulnerability, starvation, and victimization. And so to survive, Ruth visited a nearby field, walked behind the harvesters, and picked up leftover grain.

Later, she found out that the particular field in which she'd been gleaning belonged to a wealthy man named Boaz, a relative of Elimelek. Boaz looked upon Ruth with tenderness, and he protected, comforted, and watched over her. Ruth's work as a single woman was not easy, and the job she had to do to survive may have seemed humbling or demeaning. Many of you may have jobs that feel much the same. Nevertheless, Ruth pressed on, working from dawn until dusk with just one short rest (Ruth 2).

And somehow, in the midst of Ruth's wounds and her hard work, she kept herself pure and honest before the Lord.

I'll say it again—we can either run toward or away from the Lord with our wounds. In Jerry Sittser's book *A Grace Disguised*, he wrote about losing three generations of his family (his mother, wife, and daughter) in one car accident. Not long after the funeral, he had a frightening dream that he shared with his sister. He told her he had seen the sun set and ran frantically toward it before it set. All he wanted to do was to sit in the warmth of the light, but he didn't make it. His sister told him that instead of running toward the sunset, he should embrace the darkness and head in the direction of the sunrise. Jerry says that at that very moment, he understood that he had the power to choose what direction his life would take.[2]

---

2. Jerry Sittser, *A Grace Disguised* (Grand Rapids: Zondervan, 1996), 33.

When you're grieving, what kind of behavior will you choose? Will you become bitter . . . vindictive . . . even violent? Or will you let God into your wounds to speak His healing over them? Will you somehow, in the midst of your pain, turn your grief over to Him for safe-keeping? Will you surrender, and let God take care of the people or circumstances that have wounded you?

Over time, Boaz noticed something so precious in Ruth that he declared to her: "All the people of my town know that you are a woman of noble character" (3:11). Not one—all of the people in town could see Ruth's nobility. You see, unlike Naomi, whose loss made her bitter, Ruth decided to find a way to move forward with godly character. Without complaint, she rose each day and stepped into life. She committed not only to existing, but surviving. God will always honor that kind of choice—and He honored it in Ruth.

As days and months passed, Ruth found a way to love again. The very man she met in the fields became the one who would walk beside her. Boaz took her hand in marriage, and the two of them gave birth to a son, Obed. The Bible tells us that Obed's family gave birth to Jesse, and Jesse's family gave birth to David. So Ruth became the great-grandmother to the greatest king who ever ruled Israel!

Ruth couldn't foresee that losing her husband would cause her to turn from her old ways and instead follow another kind of life—and the one true God. She had no idea that God had already declared her steps, paved the way, and affirmed her value. She had no idea of the impact of her future . . . but God knew.

In *A New Time & Place*, author and pastor Jack Hayford writes, "The eternal God had a plan well beyond her scope or grasp. . . . Think of it! Baby Obed . . . that tiny package of fulfillment . . . would become a pivotal link in Almighty God's coming to earth! Obed's future grandson David would become the king of Israel, and from his seed would rise the One who, in the fullness of time, would be called 'Messiah.'"[3]

"Why Moab?" Leave it to God to take a Moabite woman who experienced such a tragic loss, bring her into the very land He promised the Israelites, and make her a descendant of the Most High King—Jesus Christ!

DENA ❦ "Leave it to God." That phrase strikes me. When we are faced with a loss that shatters our very sense of self, how do we leave it to God?

How do we love fully and well, knowing we might lose the one we love someday? And how do we comfort those who are going through the brutal separation of death, without causing them further pain?

I suffered a miscarriage early in my marriage, and it floored me that my friends and coworkers said things like, "You can always have another baby" or "You're so young" (as if that made my loss any less painful). They tried to comfort me with phrases such as, "There was probably something wrong with the baby" or "It just wasn't God's time," and while I know each person meant well, those words hurt instead of comforting me.

Our culture doesn't want to deal with death. Television, books, and movie companies make money off our fascination with vampires and zombies, but they also tell us how to add years to our life and reverse aging . . . as if we can cheat the inevitable. We are so afraid of staring death in the face. We forget that when Jesus stared down death on the cross, He took away its power . . . forever.

So we try to minimize each other's pain and—even in the church—

---

3. Jack Hayford, *A New Time & Place* (Sisters, OR: Multnomah, 1997), 111–12.

gloss over the dark, bone-crushing grief we experience with platitudes like, "It's all part of God's plan" and "He works all things for good." We don't realize that the truth of those words is overshadowed by our poor timing or our lack of sensitivity and thoughtfulness. (As my husband says, "I can't hear what you're saying because of the way you're saying it.")

I think we're simply uncomfortable around loss, as if tragedy is catching and we'll be next in line if we get too close.

A friend of mine lost her eighteen-year-old in a horrific car accident, and one of the ministers at her church said to her a few months later, "I thought you'd be better by now." As if there were statutes of limitations on grieving. As if losing a child was something akin to having surgery.

Ladies, that's not the way Jesus wants us to "do church."

He asks us to wait in the garden—not to fall asleep—to watch and pray with those who are facing tremendous grief, to the point of sweating blood. He wants us to be patient with them as they wrestle with their faith and doubt.

Can we refrain from giving easy answers, and not give up on our friends as they struggle to find solid ground again? Can we just sit with our relatives and be quiet, entering their sorrow with humility and tears? Remember—this is what Jesus did at the grave of Lazarus, whom He loved. Before He performed a miracle, before He prayed or spoke the truth through Scripture, before He displayed God's power over death, He entered the suffering of Mary and Martha.

I love this Jesus! He could have marched to the tomb and given orders, knowing that the ending would be happy. Instead, He took time to listen to His friends' questions, interact with them, and cry with them. I imagine Him reaching out His hands to pull Mary up after she had fallen to her feet in front of Him. I see Him embracing Martha after she spoke of her belief in His divinity. After all, He wasn't just the Savior of the world—He was human. And through His loving mercy in the face of earthly loss, He shows us how to be a friend to those who truly need it.

A Resurrector and Reuniter

Jesus was also passionate about bringing life, not death. Dr. Howard Batson says that Jesus never left a funeral without raising the dead to life. With His compassion and death-erasing power, He turned wakes into parties! And Batson says, Jesus wasn't discriminatory about who He chose to resurrect. Young, old, male, female . . . He raised them all: "Scriptures teach us that Jesus is a reuniter. He reunites those who are living with those who have died. And He will do the same for us, reuniting us with our sons, daughters, wives, husbands, parents, and friends—because He IS the resurrection and the life."[4]

Our world desperately needs the grave-busting hope that Jesus brings. Maybe that's why titles like *90 Minutes in Heaven* and *Heaven Is for Real* have climbed the best-seller charts (and stayed there). The success of those books shows that people have a hunger for truth and hope, especially the hope of eternal life and reunions with those we love and long for.

As the Creator, the One who set up the parameters of life and death before He formed the world, Jesus knew loss was a certainty—but He chose love (not fear or solitude). Throughout Scripture, we see God the Father and God the Son choosing love, pointing the way for us.

So the question is: will we choose love or fear? Relationship or solitude? Especially after devastating losses, will we reach out again and embrace life as the beautiful, mysterious, and ultimately worthwhile risk it is?

In *The Middle Place*, Kelly Corrigan writes of a conversation she once

---

4. Howard Batson, "Jesus, Our Hope of Resurrection" (sermon, First Baptist Church, Amarillo, Texas, February 29, 2012).

had with a Buddhist woman, Sabine, in Nepal about the "four truths" of the Buddhist faith. Kelly nodded along with the first truth, suffering is inevitable, and swallowed the second, suffering is caused by craving pleasure and avoiding what is unpleasant. But then Sabine told Kelly about the third truth, that suffering will only end when you eliminate your desires, when you break your attachments—not just to material goods, but to ideas, jobs, goals, even people.

Kelly writes, "I was proud of my attachments to people. I mean, sure, don't attach to marble countertops or the Burberry fall line. But people? I say attach, wrap around, braid yourself into. What's the point of life without attachments? We are our attachments."

When Sabine added, "Attachment turns the wheel of suffering. You can't hope to avoid suffering if you refuse to give up your attachments," Kelly decided, *Oh. Then I'll suffer. I'll choose suffering.*[5]

Attach . . . wrap around . . . braid yourself into. Hmmm . . . that sounds biblical to me! Ecclesiastes 4:12 says, "A cord of three strands is not quickly broken."

Jesus's love binds us as believers in ways we can't fully understand, at least until we reach heaven. Song of Songs 8:6–7 says, "Place me like a seal over your heart, like a seal on your arm; for love is as strong as death, its jealousy unyielding as the grave. It burns like blazing fire, like a mighty flame. Many waters cannot quench love; rivers cannot sweep it away."

I believe that those who've preceded us in death love us even better in heaven, because they don't have the baggage we have on earth. And the love we share with them will be fully realized in our eternal home, much more than it ever was on earth. How exciting!

If we allow Him to, God takes the love that weaves into and out of our lives and creates a beautiful tapestry. Love—whether it is reciprocated or not—is never wasted, because God *is* love. Doesn't Jesus say

---

5. Kelly Corrigan, *The Middle Place* (New York: Hyperion, 2008), 125.

that whatever we've done to the "least of these," we've done to Him? So even love that can't—or won't—be returned is an offering to Him, one that serves and pleases Him.

Overcoming Through and With Him

Ruth took the love she and her husband shared (and the grief that came afterward) and—instead of closing herself off—chose to open her heart once again to new places, people, and opportunities. She chose to pour herself into her mother-in-law's life and trust God with the results.

How did she do it? How can we choose life when everything in us wants to crawl in bed and never come out?

This is what Jesus meant when He said, "I am the vine; you are the branches. . . . Apart from me you can do nothing" (John 15:5).

Without Him, we can't respond lovingly when people say terrible things.

Without Him, we can't choose to attach to people like Ruth did. After all, how could she have known that going back to Israel wouldn't bring her more pain and suffering?

Without Him, we can't go on when we lose a spouse, parent, or child.

Without Him, we can't know the reality of heaven.

Without Him, we won't know the reality of a full, abundant life on earth.

"Judy" survived a horrific loss at a relatively young age. For her, too, the only hope was Jesus . . .

I always considered myself a very strong person who could act and react in emergencies with relative calm, but when my forty-year-old husband died of a massive heart attack in the kitchen of our rural home, I could not even calm myself to call 911.

One early morning in August, I heard a crash in the kitchen. When I went to see what had fallen, there on the floor beside the table lay my husband, Richard, face down on the floor. I didn't know if Richard had suffered a heart attack or a seizure, but somehow, I was able to summon an ambulance. Looking back on those first minutes, I don't remember what my two children and I were doing before the paramedics came and tried to revive Richard. It all seemed to blur together.

I didn't realize the full impact of Richard's sudden death until many days later when I began to understand that the children and I could not stay on the ranch by ourselves, especially with winter coming. My new teaching job was starting in two weeks, so it was imperative that I pull myself together, help the children deal with this incredible loss, and go on without my spouse.

The next year was full of numerous adjustments: a hurried move to a home in the small town near my children's school, waves of grief and anger over being left alone with a multitude of decisions to make. I remember crying all the way to school only to put on my professional face and teach the students as if I had it all together. My children both acted out their grief and anger in their own ways, and for the first time in my life, I was shocked to find myself, a mature Christian, on the mental health hotline crying desperately for help to pull it together.

It has taken years for us to adjust. My teenage daughter tried to fill the void in her life by seesawing between rebellion and perfectionism. My young son erupted in anger over every difficult thing he couldn't fix himself. I poured myself into my job with a vengeance, because it seemed to be the only area where I was still in some semblance of control.

God was so gracious during all this turmoil and walked us through the valleys that seemed too dark to navigate alone; but being single in my late thirties was never a place I wanted to walk, even with God beside me.

Now that I've experienced the challenges of remarriage, blending two families, and helping adult children find their way in life, I look back with a sigh and say, "You've come a long way, baby!" It's all by the grace of God. There are still moments, for all three of us, when we experience grief and sadness, but there are great memories of Richard that we can still share. We might be laughing or crying when we reminisce—but one thing's for sure: we are overcomers.

Sweet friends, this is my prayer for every woman who's been wounded (which means all of us): I pray that we will not let our losses shut us off from living, but that we will be overcomers. Can I pray for us right now?

God, make us women who overcome fear and reach expectantly for love. Help us trust You for the grace to do this. May we remain in Christ and let Him live His death-busting and love-multiplying life through us. Grant us the grace and courage to share the hope He gives us with others, so that they, too, can overcome the world. In Jesus's name, amen.

5

Hagar

From Persecuted to Pursued

❀ GENESIS 16 ❀

TINA ❧ Beautiful Sarah must have paced back and forth a
hundred times, wringing her hands. She wanted to be the one to have
Abraham's children; she wanted to conceive. Her thoughts raced
toward glances and whispers she'd so often received from others.
Shame and guilt over her infertility draped her soul as she continued to
pace. Earlier, during Abraham's quiet time with the Lord, God spoke
to him and promised him an heir from his own flesh and blood. Did he
share that with Sarah? Sarah had carried the wound of infertility long
enough. In her eyes it was time for desperate measures. After many
years of waiting to conceive a child, she decided to give her maidservant,
Hagar, to her beloved husband.

The Maidservant

What did the moment look like when Sarah finally decided to give
her maidservant to Abraham? In order to understand the story more
fully, let's start from the beginning.

Many years prior to this moment, during a severe famine, Abraham took his family and traveled to Egypt to live. During that time, Abraham was called Abram and Sarah was called Sarai. God later changed their names to what we now call them today—Abraham and Sarah. Before entering the city, he said to Sarai (Sarah), "I know what a beautiful woman you are. When the Egyptians see you, they will say, 'This is his wife.' Then they will kill me but will let you live. Say you are my sister, so that I will be treated well for your sake and my life will be spared because of you" (Gen. 12:11–13).

Just as Abraham predicted, when Pharaoh's officials saw Sarah, they praised her, and she was taken into Pharaoh's palace. "He treated Abram [Abraham] well for her sake; and gave him sheep and oxen and donkeys and male and *female servants* and female donkeys and camels" (v. 16 NASB, emphasis added). Perhaps this is when Abraham and Sarah acquired Hagar, who Scripture tells us was Egyptian (Gen. 16:3). Even as a slave, she would have been accustomed to a different way of life than the nomadic lifestyle of Abraham and Sarah. Egypt itself was far advanced in its economic system, as well as its religious order. For Hagar to become a slave in a nomadic family meant that she would travel quite a bit, living outside the security of solid walls and having to learn new skills for survival. She would also learn of a God her culture did not worship.

Pharaoh soon learned the truth that Sarah was, indeed, Abraham's wife—not his sister. He gave Sarah back to Abraham and sent all of them away. The Bible gives no record of whether Abraham left the gifts given to him from Pharaoh behind. Scripture says only that "Pharaoh gave orders about Abram to his men, and they sent him on his way, with his wife and everything he had" (v. 20). "Everything" likely included Hagar.

A Slave's Duty

Back to the moment we imagined earlier. Sarah finally approached Abraham and said, "The LORD has kept me from having children. Go, sleep with my slave; perhaps I can build a family through her" (16:2).

There's no account of any discussion; only that Abraham simply agreed to Sarah's request. "So after Abram had been living in Canaan ten years, Sarai his wife took her Egyptian slave Hagar and gave her to her husband to be his wife" (v. 3).

Just as Sarah desired, Abraham and Hagar conceived a child. Unfortunately, "when [Hagar] knew she was pregnant, she began to despise her mistress" (v. 4). In other words, Hagar treated Sarah with less respect—and Sarah noticed.

When the Bible speaks of slaves, it often doesn't give insight into how they felt about their duties. More than likely, they were encouraged to simply perform their tasks and were prohibited from speaking openly. But they were still human beings. They may not have been worth much to their masters, but to the Lord they had great value.

Surely Hagar had her own thoughts about being sent out of the comfort of the familiar and thrust into the hands of nomads. Along with that, she was now forced into motherhood, knowing she would give birth and care for a child who would belong to Sarah. Did she relish the idea of conceiving a child with the leader of a great tribe, knowing it would elevate her social status? Or did she despise the very thought of it? Was her disrespect toward Sarah due to disgust at the action she must take, or did she become proud?

The Wound—Mistreated

Often times, when our speech is stifled, our emotions surface in other ways. We understand this, ladies. Sometimes it is difficult to find words in the middle of our most sensitive moments. How do we sort through our sea of feelings, find our voice, and speak the truth in love? With God's help, we can find a way.

Perhaps Hagar stuffed her feelings down and the emotions surfaced as derision. As for Sarah, if she was like most people, she needed someone to blame for how she was feeling. And Sarah blamed Abraham.

Can't we relate, ladies? Don't we, at times, tend to blame our husbands for our emotions?

> Then Sarah said to Abram, "You are responsible for the wrong I am suffering. I put my slave in your arms, and now that she knows she is pregnant, she despises me. May the LORD judge between you and me." (v. 5)

Sarah's anger roared throughout the camp. If she could take her fury out on Abraham in such a way, what could she do to Hagar?

"'Your slave is in your hands,' Abram said. 'Do with her whatever you think best'" (v. 6). Abraham deftly avoided the issue and handed it back to Sarah. And rightly so, because Sarah, as the wife of the leader of the tribe, would have been in charge of the women of the tribe.

How long did it take Sarah to confront Hagar after speaking with her husband? Scripture doesn't tell us; it only says, "Then Sarai mistreated Hagar; so she fled from her" (v. 6). *Sarah mistreated Hagar.* In what way? What did she say? How did she do it? Imagine a woman filled with bitterness and anger, racing toward another, ready to unload. Have you been there?

As I write, I am reminded of a wounding moment regarding my own heart; a moment I felt mistreated. I don't remember why I was fighting with my husband, only the impact of his words. My sons were young— one a baby and the other a toddler. All I wanted to do was go home to my parents, or anywhere other than where I stood. I raced to load the kids and start the car. Nothing happened. I turned the key and my heart sank when I heard *click click.* The car would not start. In my younger years, I didn't recognize that perhaps God was trying to tell me something. I ignored the message and plunged forward with my own plans, calling and asking a friend to jump-start the car. There we were, two young women (one a pastor's wife), in the dark, trying to connect the cables. At some point I must have confessed why I was in such a hurry to leave.

I remember my friend boasting, "Tina, I feel like I'm breaking you out of jail!"

I shouted, "You are!"

Needless to say, I didn't go far; God brought me back.

The very word *mistreated* takes us back to a time in our own lives when we suffered such a wound. And however the scene unfolded, it must have been a very heated confrontation. It caused Hagar to flee from Sarah and venture out into the desert—alone. Like many women faced with wounded hearts, she just wanted to go home. She traveled down a common road used by traders, which led her through the wilderness and along the Shur Desert. It would have been strenuous travel for anyone, especially a pregnant woman. Nevertheless, Hagar's wound drove her farther and farther along the desert road.

Where have your wounds taken you? What terrain have you traversed just to get away from the pain? As I sit and ponder the image of women all over the world traveling difficult paths, hoping the road will carry them to safe places, my heart aches. Some women probably have no idea they are even running.

The God Who Sees

Hagar stumbled to the spring and splashed water on her parched lips. It trickled down her burning neck and soaked her collar. Taking hold of the hem of her dress, she dipped it in the cool stream and wiped her dirty face. Strands of hair fell on her sweaty brow. Tired and weary, she gently brushed them aside, exhaled a deep sigh, and looked out at the vast desert.

Startled by a voice, she quickly turned to see an angel standing before her. He said: "Hagar, slave of Sarai, where have you come from, and where are you going?"

"I'm running away from my mistress Sarai," she answered. Then the angel of the LORD told her, "Go back to your mistress and submit to her" (vv. 8–9).

Can't you just visualize the shock and fear on Hagar's face?

You want me to do what?

The angel added, "I will increase your descendants so much that they will be too numerous to count" (v. 10).

The promise was tantalizing, but Hagar's wound was still fresh. There was no time to heal, and yet the Lord was asking her to go back and submit to Sarah.

Then the angel said, "You are now pregnant and you will give birth to a son. You shall name him Ishmael, for the LORD has heard of your misery" (v. 11).

In that moment, she heard the angel say something profound: *The Lord has heard of your misery.* Remember your own wounded times of feeling alone . . . and at just the right moment, someone came to comfort, embrace, hold, and affirm you. God sent an angel to let Hagar know that He hears . . . He sees . . . He cares.

A slave woman accustomed to Egypt's gods and ways, in the presence of the Lord's messenger, felt the love of the God she had not known. Tired from her travels and deeply wounded, she now found herself at a place of complete brokenness. What would she do? What would become of her and her child? She longed to go back to a place that seemed familiar and safe; yet the Lord was asking her to do something that felt completely perilous.

Hagar, in the middle of the desert, had an epiphany. An overwhelming presence fell upon her, and for the first time in her life, she understood something—God sees. "You are the God who sees me," she said. "I have now seen the One who sees me" (v. 13).

What an incredible moment it is when we realize God is ever-present in our life! Hagar's revelation gave her the courage to turn and make the long journey back to Sarah. It gave her the courage to face the one who had wounded her, knowing it might happen again. It gave her the courage to do the right thing, knowing she did not have to rest in her strength alone. She knew that the God who sees would take care of her and her child. But the greatest insight of all in Hagar's wounded moment was that *she* saw. Not only did she understand that God sees, but her eyes were opened to see Him as well.

DENA ❀ Want to know something amazing? Hagar was the only woman in the Scriptures to name God. She saw Him for who He really was, and called Him "Elohim" (the God who sees me). In the midst of a dry, barren desert, "Hagar's extremity became God's opportunity."[1]

From her desperate encounter, Hagar received a sense of God's provision and protection. And God ultimately blessed her obedience, just as He will bless us when we obey. However, it's not easy to trust God when He's leading us to do something more difficult than we could ever imagine. In order to change our character and heighten our dependence on Him, He may ask us to surrender our long-cherished dreams, ideas, or habits. He may even ask us to remain in a job, relationship, or place that has caused us pain.

Why? God knows when our plans, dreams, and rituals have turned into idols. He sees us relying on other things and people for comfort and relief, and He wants to guide us to a place of freedom instead of bondage. So He whispers to us: *Trust Me. Open your palms and release what you're grasping tightly. I promise that I will hold onto you and sustain you, if you will just give Me everything.*

---

1. From Bible Gateway's "Women of the Bible" 6/4/12 devotional on Hagar, http://www.biblegateway.org. Excerpt taken from Herbert Lockyer's "All the Women of the Bible," copyright 1967.

A Mean Mother-in-Law

By email, my friend Morningstar told me that her mother-in-law had repeatedly berated her through both words and actions. "I was going through a stressful time, and I packed on some pounds," she wrote. "One day my mother-in-law brought out a picture of me that was taken several months earlier. She said, 'I want you to look at this picture. You don't look good at all! You have gained too much weight.' As many women will attest to, it's unexpected, spiteful words that hurt the most."

Another time, Morningstar made a lovely Thanksgiving meal for her mother-in-law and part of her family. "She said very little during the meal except to say toward the end of the meal, 'You shouldn't serve nut bread with the meal. That should be for dessert. That's just not the way it's done!' Again, she smiled because she knew it would hurt me."

After suffering even more wounds, Morningstar believed God was asking her to love and pray for her mother-in-law. She said, "After many years of wanting to get back at her for all the nasty things she said and did to me (and my husband), I finally knelt down and asked God to heal me. It was a struggle to come to God for this kind of help. I don't know why I waited so long . . . my stubborn spirit had kept me in bondage. When I finally got on my knees, I said, 'Lord Jesus, help me! I can't stand feeling this way anymore! Help me to forgive her, Lord, and let me move on. She needs Your help, Lord, because she is angry at the world.'"

God's healing didn't come overnight, but eventually Morningstar felt release and joy. She wrote, "Recently, my mother-in-law fell down and injured herself. She suffered alone for two days and could have died. Now, it looks like she will be laid up for quite some time. My husband and I went to see her, and we weren't sure what to expect. But as soon as she saw us come in the hospital room, her eyes lit up—she smiled and welcomed us in! We're hoping that she has turned to Christ and will live a more godly and loving life."

Morningstar learned firsthand that the time we have with others is relatively short, and God doesn't want us to waste our lives holding on to bitterness and anger: "It's so important to savor each day and stay close to Christ. We all have a choice—to be a positive, loving person or a negative, unloving person. No matter how you're treated, someone else's negativity has nothing to do with you and everything to do with them."

She noted several actions that help her stay focused on Christ: reading her Bible each day, praying for herself and others, and releasing her worries to Him. As she meditates on God's character and sees Him more clearly, she is able to continue praying for her mother-in-law, instead of rehearsing resentments.

What difficult thing is God calling you to do?

Raise a teen who daily—or hourly—spews hateful words at you?

Show Jesus's love to a demeaning boss?

Start a ministry when you've been wounded in the same type of outreach before?

Stay married to a spouse who continually disappoints you?

Remain in a city where you feel invisible and alone?

I urge you to trust Him . . . no matter what. Let your extremity become His opportunity! You may not understand why He's asking you to obey, and you may be unsure how long you'll have to remain in a difficult situation. But whatever you go through, He promises to sustain you. He will never leave you to fend for yourself. Run to Him, and let Him show you *His* plans and purposes. He longs to open your eyes to see Him, to make you aware of His presence.

Hearing God in the Silence

A dear friend and former newspaper reporter, Jennifer Lee wrestled for years with anxiety and perfectionism, keeping busy so she wouldn't have to face the gaping hole in her heart. But God met her and slowed her down, teaching her to rest and wait. Here's her story:

My deepest fear was that if left alone, I'd be deafened by silence. So I would put my world on maximum volume with the *click-click* of my high heels and the fast scratching of pencils at press conferences. I lived a megaphone life, afraid that in the silence I'd be faced with the gripping pain of my doubt.

I chased front-page stories, and byline glory, and surrounded myself with the noise of me, me, me. I was afraid that in the silence, my deepest doubts would scream loud like this: God is not real!

I feared that the absence of sound would prove the absence of God.

What if I asked Him in the silence to speak to me? And then, what if . . . ?

What if?

What if I heard only my own desperate breathing?

But some questions are worth the risk of "what if."

For I found the answer in the silence, with my soul laid bare five years ago on the floor of my bedroom closet. (Me, like a filthy rag next to the dirty-clothes hamper.) In the quiet, I asked the question.

My sister was there helping me during a rough time after the birth of our second child. She says I looked different when I walked out of the bedroom that day. That's because I'd heard Him whisper in the Spirit voice: *I am real.*

I no longer fear the silence of hours. Even more, I no longer fear the silence of God. I speak to Him, and sometimes hear only this . . .

Silence.

Even still, even silent, I know He's here.

Oh yes, He's here.

Just as God made His presence known to Hagar and Jennifer, He longs to make His presence known to you. He wants us to come to Him with our wounds, so that He can touch and restore us. His tender heart aches when ours bleed.

Though others may slander us, He soothes.

Though hurtful words may cause our hearts to break, He heals.

Though people may accuse, attack, or shun us, He never will. He is the God of comfort and peace, with whom we have no reason to be afraid.

Finally Free

Hagar submitted to God and returned to Sarah, but that wasn't the end of her story. She gave birth to a son, Ishmael, and remained a faithful servant to her masters. During the next ten years, she witnessed the fulfillment of God's promise in the birth of Isaac to Sarah and Abraham.

> The child grew and was weaned, and on the day Isaac was weaned Abraham held a great feast. But Sarah saw that the son whom Hagar the Egyptian had borne to Abraham was mocking, and she said to Abraham, "Get rid of that slave woman and her son, for that woman's son will never share in the inheritance with my son Isaac." (Gen. 21:8–10)

Sarah's request bothered Abraham, because Ishmael was not just Hagar's offspring—he was Abraham's son too. (Notice Sarah didn't even use Hagar's or Ishmael's names. Instead, she called them "that slave woman and her son.") But God told Abraham not to worry. He promised to make both sons into great nations.

The story continues:

> Early the next morning Abraham took some food and a skin of water and gave them to Hagar. He set them on her shoulders

and then sent her off with the boy. She went on her way and
wandered in the Desert of Beersheba.

When the water in the skin was gone, she put the boy under
one of the bushes. Then she went off and sat down about a
bowshot away, for she thought, "I cannot watch the boy die."
And as she sat there, she began to sob.

God heard the boy crying, and the angel of God called
to Hagar from heaven and said to her, "What is the matter,
Hagar? Do not be afraid; God has heard the boy crying as he
lies there. Lift the boy up and take him by the hand, for I will
make him into a great nation."

Then God opened her eyes and she saw a well of water.
So she went and filled the skin with water and gave the boy a
drink.

God was with the boy as he grew up. (vv. 14–20)

Once again, Hagar ended up in the desert. This time, she didn't leave
of her own volition. Instead, Sarah—jealous and fearful of Ishmael's
claim on her son Isaac's inheritance—insisted that Abraham send
Hagar away.

Sitting in the dust of the desert, Hagar experienced desolation.
Like Jennifer, she sat in the silence. And in the silence she began to cry,
because she believed she and her son would die. Can you imagine having to watch your only child die of thirst? I can't fathom being in such a
heart-wrenching situation.

Then God, who would watch His only Son hang naked—in extreme
thirst—on the cross, heard the boy's cry. And in compassion and mercy,
just as He had once before, God used an angel to minister to Hagar and
Ishmael. The angel spoke to her, God opened her eyes, and she found
a well.

Oh, friend, God is real. God sees. He hears our cries—and our children's cries. Our pain and distress move Him to action. The psalmist

David writes, "You, God, are my God, earnestly I seek you; I thirst for you, my whole being longs for you, in a dry and parched land where there is no water" (Ps. 63:1).

In the midst of our desperation, God delivers. Sometimes, He shows us a simple way to meet a physical need that's causing us pain. At other times, He gives us guidance through people who encourage us with words of truth and strength. Always, He provides Scripture to fill our spiritual hunger, and Jesus, the Living Water, to quench our thirst. Psalm 107:9 says, "He satisfies the thirsty and fills the hungry with good things."

He filled Hagar and her son with physical water, meeting their immediate needs. And He protected them and guided them, meeting their long-term needs for safety and shelter. A few years after they left Abraham and Sarah's service, God led Hagar to find a wife for her son. And eventually, He made Ishmael the father of twelve nations (like Israel). I'm sure Hagar enjoyed her many grandchildren and great-grandchildren.

Our heavenly Father kept His promises to Hagar . . . and He keeps His promises to us. I love what Mary Beth Chapman says: "In the midst of it all, God really is with us and for us. I have found that even during those times when the path is darkest, He leaves little bits of evidence all along the way—bread crumbs of grace—that can give me what I need to take the next step. But I can only find them if I choose to SEE."[2]

What if Jennifer hadn't slowed down to hear God? What if fear about what she might hear, or *not* hear, kept her from the bedroom closet? Would she have had health problems, exacerbated by stress? Would her career have continued to flourish, at the expense of her family? Or would she have continued to feel driven and desperate, refusing to turn to God and becoming increasingly depressed over time?

---

2. Mary Beth Chapman, with Ellen Vaughn, *Choosing to SEE: A Journey of Struggle and Hope* (Grand Rapids: Revell, 2010), 26.

Sometimes the natural consequences of our "me, me, me" choices catch up with us. But it doesn't have to be that way.

Instead of continuing to run, Jennifer hungered and thirsted for Him, pouring out her soul. He met her at the point of her need, and He continues to do so. I met Jennifer through The High Calling, a ministry for which we both write and edit. I've watched her grow—and glow!—in His Spirit as she pours out the Living Water to hundreds of thirsty followers at her own blog,[3] on various websites, and in an upcoming book project with Tyndale House.

Each day, we can ask God for His perspective, determine to obey what He calls us to do, and honestly share our hunger and thirst with Him. If we live with ears tuned to the Spirit's voice, and eyes open to see His workings in the world, each day will unfold in startling—and extremely satisfying—ways. Eventually, like Hagar, when we see Him clearly, we can obey quickly and without question. Our lives then become a living, dynamic portrait of God's presence, promises, and power.

Am I truly open to this way of living? I hope so. Are you? I pray so. Though it's not "natural," walking hand in hand with our Maker (instead of running ahead or lagging behind Him) is liberating. And joyous!

Let me testify as one who has struggled, and continues to struggle, with completely giving over her plans to God: It gets easier and sweeter all the time. Each time we exercise our trust in God, our faith "muscles" get a little stronger. He shows His trustworthiness, and we believe more fully. He gently leads us to the point of full surrender and unquestioning belief in His goodness. And as our faith increases, so does our joy. At the same time, peace takes over our lives and anxiety flees. Author and speaker Tammy Maltby writes, "The testimony of Hagar is that we *can* 'see' the God who sees us. We can be aware of His presence, of what He is doing in the world and our lives. That's the testimony of the Bible.

---

3. http://www.gettingdownwithjesus.blogspot.com.

And even though I've spent my share of days squinting into the fog, it's my testimony too."[4]

Here's something else amazing about Hagar's story. The first time she left Sarah and Abraham's camp—a decision she made out of woundedness—she left as a slave. She took nothing, because she had no possessions. As we've learned, God met her in the wilderness and gave her His strength to return as a slave. Over a decade passed as she obediently served her masters (and her Master).

The second time she journeyed out of the camp—through no fault of her own—she left with her freedom. No longer would she answer to an earthly master; she belonged to God alone!

What a stunning, perfect picture of God's grace. Through our own and others' failings, we suffer wounds. But if we cry out to Him, Jesus meets us at the point of our need. He provides daily sustenance for our souls. Over time, He gives us complete and total freedom. And as we mature in Him, we hear His voice more clearly and revel in the truth of His promises. In turn, we can lead others to Him, so they can find freedom.

Praise His holy name!

May we become wounded-but-healing women who live with eyes and hearts open to God's purposes: "This resurrection life you received from God is not a timid, grave-tending life. It's adventurously expectant, greeting God with a childlike 'What's next, Papa?' God's Spirit touches our spirits and confirms who we really are. We know who he is, and we know who we are: Father and children" (Rom. 8:15–16 MSG).

4. Tammy Maltby, *The God Who Sees You* (Colorado Springs: David C. Cook, 2012), 72.

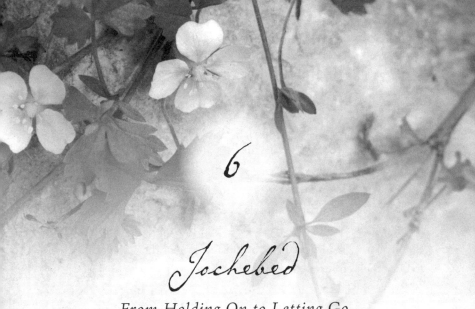

6

Jochebed

From Holding On to Letting Go

✺ EXODUS 2 ✺

TINA ✺ Casey and her husband walked through the doors carrying their newborn son. Doctors told her that the child would only live a few days. Days turned into weeks, and months passed. The clock seemed to stand still as we all watched and prayed. Was time the enemy—or a gift? At three months old, Joshua's life on earth came to an end.

Writing this chapter hit close to home. Casey and Jochebed, an Israelite woman, share a common thread—they both had to release their babies at three months of age.

Pharaoh, the king of Egypt, had demanded that all male babies be thrown into the Nile River. I can't imagine what the Nile River looked like—or the faces of the mothers who watched their babies drown. It was a wound not many of us can fathom.

I can't imagine how Jochebed or my friend must have felt after having their sons. Think of their joy, and then the shocking realization their child would die. Neither one of them could protect their sons, or hold on to them any longer. What an extremely painful wound!

An Emotional Release

I've never had to go through the agony of losing a child from a miscarriage or death, but I've listened to the cries and heard the painful stories of my friends who've had to endure such tragedies.

One friend's son served overseas in the military, only to come home and be killed in a car accident two weeks later. I saw the pain and suffering my mother endured over the loss of my brother—her son. Watching them, I struggled mightily with the fact that mothers sometimes have to bury their children. It seems unfair and cruel.

Before my father's death, he shared a heart-wrenching story with me that I'll never forget. I had a sister who was a year older than me. She had black hair, bright blue eyes, and beautiful porcelain skin. Three days after she came home from the hospital, she stopped breathing. My father shared how he tried to bring her back to life: He cupped her tiny frame in his large hands and ran to the car. He then cracked the window on the driver's side of the vehicle and held her limp body up to it—hoping that the cool wind on her face would miraculously cause her to start breathing again. Finally, he sped into the parking lot of the nearest hospital and ran inside, still clinging to the lifeless body of his tiny daughter. The nurses and the doctors didn't even look at the baby. They turned him away and declared that they could not help him because he didn't have insurance and because they were a private hospital. I ache at the thought of my father and mother carrying such a wound.

I've listened to friends talk about losing their children either because of sin or through devastating circumstances. Losing a child to an addiction, for instance, can feel just as painful as losing them through death. One grandmother shared how she had to track down her fourteen-year-old drug-addicted grandson, who lived on the streets.

I've also heard stories of mothers grieving because their children don't want anything to do with them, or with God.

It comforts me to know that the Lord hears the cries of His children calling out to Him on behalf of their own children. He does not leave them alone.

From Abraham, who took his son to be sacrificed on the altar, to Bathsheba, who lost her firstborn from an illness, the Lord has heard the cries of His children. He heard the cry of the wealthy man whose son chose to leave, live a life of sin, and squander his inheritance. God heard the cries of Mary, whom He appointed to be the mother of His own Son, Jesus . . . who was beaten, bludgeoned, and crucified on the cross. The Lord heard the cries of His people, and He has heard our cries for our own children.

Jochebed, in desperation, chose to risk everything and attempt to keep her child hidden until three months had passed. Finally, time ran out. Whether he got too big to hide, or whether her neighbors became suspicious, Scripture doesn't say. It does say: "When she could hide him no longer, she got a papyrus basket for him and coated it with tar and pitch. Then she placed the child in it and put it among the reeds along the bank of the Nile" (Exod. 2:3).

Jochebed knew that holding on to her child would not prevent his death . . . and it might possibly bring death to her and the rest of her family. So she did as Pharaoh commanded and put her son in the Nile River—but she did it in her own way. Out of all the Israelite mothers, was Jochebed the only one who thought of such a clever plan?

Jochebed gently laid her baby in the basket and firmly tucked the cloth around him. She placed the basket in the water, holding tight until she felt it was secure enough to float on its own. Then she released it. In that moment, she not only thrust her child into the unknown, she also released him into the arms of the God of Abraham, Isaac, and Jacob.

I wonder, how did Jochebed finally surrender her child? And what emotions did she feel as she released him?

As Jochebed stood at a distance and watched the basket float away, her daughter Miriam followed behind. Can't you see Miriam, the diligent older sister, scurrying behind the basket and watching attentively?

As the basket gently floated, it got caught on reeds in the place Pharaoh's daughter bathed.

> His sister stood at a distance to see what would happen to him.
> Then Pharaoh's daughter went down to the Nile to bathe, and her attendants were walking along the riverbank. She saw the basket among the reeds and sent her female slave to get it. She opened it and saw the baby. He was crying, and she felt sorry for him. "This is one of the Hebrew babies," she said.
> Then his sister asked Pharaoh's daughter, "Shall I go and get one of the Hebrew women to nurse the baby for you?"
> "Yes, go," she answered. So the girl went and got the baby's mother. (vv. 4–8)

What bravery and quick thinking Miriam exhibited as she stepped forward and approached the princess! In a sense, she helped save her brother's life. Did Jochebed know where the waters led? Was this her plan all along?

There comes a time when every parent has to let a child go. The letting go will look and feel different for each of us.

I remember the day my oldest son left home for the very first time. I anxiously counted the days. *Time is running out,* I would often say to myself. As the time for him to leave got closer, I realized that I had a women's retreat that I needed to attend the very weekend he was leaving. *How did that happen?* I thought.

But rather than saying, "This is a mess," I reasoned that everything fell into place the way it was supposed to. God knew better than I did, and He knew I needed to say my good-byes and then have something to distract me for a few days.

Releasing my son was sweet, but difficult. I woke him early that morning. I didn't want to release my grasp as I held his cheek to mine. Tears ran between our cheeks. I knew I would see him again, but he was moving several states away. I couldn't follow him like Miriam. I couldn't watch him float away (or even fly away) like Jochebed. I simply had to trust and let go. It was painful.

An Unexpected Return

"Momma! Come quickly! He will live, Momma! He will live!" Miriam may have shouted. Can't you picture that moment and see Jochebed's ecstatic face upon hearing Miriam's words?

Jochebed hurried to the banks of the Nile River outside of the palace, threw herself at the feet of the princess, and out of the corner of her eye caught a glimpse of her son.

Can you imagine the pounding of Jochebed's heart as her son came closer and closer and was finally placed in her arms? Choking back sobs of joy, she hears the words, "Take this baby and nurse him for me, and I will pay you" (v. 9).

A miracle of grace and love was extended to Jochebed that day. The Lord had returned her son (who would be named Moses) to her. Not only had God given Moses back to Jochebed, but she would be paid for taking care of her own flesh and blood. I can hear the proud and relieved mom laughing with her daughter as they took Moses home. Imagine Miriam shouting, "Can you believe it? God be praised!"

I love that Jochebed released her son with wisdom and courage, in the best way she knew how. And I love that she trusted in the God of Abraham, Isaac, and Jacob . . . the One who would ultimately determine Moses's steps.

The miraculous return of Jochebed's son was nothing short of what the Lord does for us.

When Abraham made his way up the mountain to build an altar and sacrifice his son, Isaac asked, "'The fire and wood are here, . . . but where is the lamb for the burnt offering?' Abraham answered, 'God himself will provide the lamb for the burnt offering, my son.' And the two of them went on together" (Gen. 22:7–8). And just as Abraham predicted, the Lord called his name right before he thrust the dagger into Isaac. Abraham looked up, and in the thicket was a ram. God provided the sacrifice and returned Isaac to Abraham.

When Bathsheba mourned the loss of her child, David went to comfort her, and in the midst of that loss, she conceived another child who would be called Solomon. He would one day become the king of Israel.

The wealthy man rose every morning hoping to see his lost son walking the road that led to his house and " . . . while [the son] was still a long way off, his father saw him and was filled with compassion for him; he ran to his son, threw his arms around him and kissed him" (Luke 15:20). The son returned home!

Mary, the mother of Jesus, watched her son die a cruel, demeaning death. But three days later, He returned by rising from the grave.

"So [Jochebed] took the baby and nursed him. When the child grew older, she took him to Pharaoh's daughter and he became her son. She named him Moses, saying, 'I drew him out of the water'" (Exod. 2:9–10).

God gave Jochebed back her son for just a short season. That's how it is with us and our children. The Lord gives them to us for a time, and then we must find a way to release them back to Him.

Whether we've lost a child through death, sin, or just through the healthy process of growing up and leaving home, we can find comfort from Jochebed's oh-so-human experience. We'll need to release them over and over again. There will be days when our hearts will feel like bursting from the loss. Sometimes, we'll cling to the pain, memories, and wound of losing someone we love so much, but all is not lost. If we turn to the Lord like Jochebed did, we will experience His strength, peace, and reassurance. There will be days when our hearts find great comfort because God has comforted us in the midst of our letting go.

Some children may never be returned to us until we embrace them in heaven. With others, we may never see them again due to the lifestyle they choose to live. And there will be those who, like the prodigal child, find their way home.

If we can learn to release to God what is already His, if for no other reason than because it is the right thing to do, then one day, we'll receive a return on what we've lost . . . a return that only God can give. With His help, we'll find a greater ability to trust deeply, love freely, and let go when the time comes. Perhaps we'll be able to minister to someone else going through a similar tragedy. Maybe the return will be a passion to start a foundation that will go on to help millions of others. Or it might simply be a change in our own life that we never expected. Whatever the return, our suffering will not go unnoticed. And God's love? No one can fathom the depth of it. Embrace it; take hold of it; allow Him to drape you in a veil of peace.

DENA ❧ I sat on the couch, my swollen body aching as I held my newborn son. Jordan slept soundly, tucked into my arm. I traced his lips, nose, and cheeks with my finger and marveled at his long eyelashes and soft skin.

Jordan's birth had come after a miscarriage, and even though he was only a few days old, I was utterly smitten. Nothing could have prepared me for the way I would feel when I looked at him. I didn't want to let him out of my sight, even for a minute.

As I held him, though, my thoughts began to wander. I realized that soon, I would need to leave him in the nursery while I sang in the choir. Later, I'd have to drop him off at kindergarten, where he'd be for *hours* . . . with a strange woman. By the time he was sixteen, he'd be driving away with strange women. And one day, in the not-so-distant future, he would marry SOMEONE ELSE.

Suddenly, my husband walked into the room. Carey smiled sweetly at me, kissed the baby, and asked, "What are you thinking?"

I exclaimed, "He's going to grow up and leave me!"

Carey's eyes widened. "Honey," he said, glancing around the room as if looking for an escape route, "It's going to be okay."

God's Constancy for Life's Changes

I've heard it said that the only certain things in life are death and taxes. I'd like to add one to that list. After forty-odd years on the planet, I can say with conviction that the only certain things in life are death, taxes, and change.

The baby I wrote about? He's now taller than me, and almost ready to get his learner's permit. Even though there were more than a few sleep-deprived days when I wanted to throttle the older ladies in Wal-Mart who told me, "Enjoy every minute—it goes so fast," it really did happen sooner than I would have liked. (At certain times, though, when he's acting like his dad and I are the biggest idiots he's ever met, I'm ready for him to drive away . . . at least for an hour or two.) All in all, I'm thankful I still have three more years before he leaves for college. My tenderhearted friend Karen Sawyer has had a very difficult time with her two children getting older. Her kids, a boy and a girl, are only two years and one school grade apart, and will be graduating from high school soon, leaving her with an empty—and very quiet—nest.

"I can barely think about it without crying," she said. "My tears are a combination of worry, missing them before they're even gone, and grieving the fact that my main job for the last eighteen years is rapidly coming to an end."

But in the midst of her struggle, God sent Karen two messages that helped her put the season of letting go in perspective. First, she heard a young NFL quarterback talk at a sports banquet. He spoke about how hard his first two years in the NFL had been and how he had even questioned if he was supposed to be there. He occasionally wondered where God was.

"But then he realized that it had been the Lord all along, giving him the strength to carry on, to witness in a tough situation," Karen told me. "He said he *had* to run to Jesus because when things got tough, quite frankly, where else was he going to go? Eventually he came to the conclusion that if it was all taken away from him today and Jesus was all he had, it would be enough. Then he challenged the audience, if everything immediately changed and all that you loved was suddenly taken away, would Jesus be enough? It started me thinking."

The very next morning, Karen's pastor preached on making our children into idols. He spoke about living vicariously through them and micromanaging their lives. Karen felt convicted as the pastor asked his congregation, "Do we put our children above God? Do we believe that we have to be in control of their lives for them to be safe, healthy, and successful? Are we helicopter parents, continually hovering? And if so, what would it take for us to trust God with our children and give control back to Him concerning our children?"

The quarterback's words and her pastor's words echoed through Karen's head as the messages mingled together. She asked herself, "Is Jesus really enough? Can He fill my empty heart when my kids are gone? Can He take care of them better than I can? If something were to happen to them, would He really be enough then?"

Through these two men's words, the Lord ministered hope and peace to Karen. God let her know that yes, He is enough—and will continue to be enough when her kids are gone, and if bad things happened. "It may be a minute-by-minute process, but I will keep my eyes on Him . . . and when my mind starts to wander and I start to worry about my kids, I will remind myself who is on the throne and that He will always be enough," she explained.

And as she "looks forward" to the future, she's learning to trust that

God has a plan not just for her children, but for her, as well: "What it really boils down to is what am I going to do and what am I going to be when they leave? While I am still their mom, my role has changed. I am no longer in charge of their lives."

Gradually, and with many tears and prayers, Karen has come to the realization that she was never really in total control anyway. God is in control, and He won't cease to be just because her situation has changed.

"It doesn't mean there won't be ups and downs and snags along the way, but He created them and He can certainly guide, direct, and manage them much better than I have ever done. And just because my kids will be gone doesn't mean my life is over. It's hard for me to imagine that anything can come close to being a mom—but who am I to say God can't out-do Himself?!"

Parenting Adult Children

Some parents let go, only to see their children make difficult choices and turn their backs on the God who loves them and wants the best for them. Perhaps we've let our children go—but God's plan for them is not what we expected. How do we deal with the grief that comes from watching our children suffer?

One mom—we'll call her "Connie"—is a single parent of two daughters. She sought to make the Lord her husband and to raise her daughters to love Jesus. Both girls are now grown with children, but neither follows the Lord. Her oldest daughter, a single parent, works full time while fighting relapsing-remitting multiple sclerosis.

"Every time she has a relapse and is unable to walk without a cane, she experiences excruciating nerve and muscle pain beyond imagination. I plead with Jesus for her healing, but even more for her trust in Him. It is a sword through my heart," Connie says.

Her youngest daughter has battled with mental illness, drug addiction, and an inconsistent relationship with Jesus. She has had two children, neither of whom she has raised. Connie says, "Every time she walks away from Jesus and goes on a drug binge, another sword pierces my heart."

Connie has bent over backward to try to fix things for her daughters: "I allowed myself to be their scapegoat, believing everything was my fault. It has taken many years and many tears and much time spent on my face, prostrate before the Lord, to realize that my daughters have free will. We all have free will."

Like many of us, Connie struggles daily to yield herself to God's will for her life. She says she is challenged every day not only to believe *in* God, but to believe *Him*.

"I know that His Word says that He desires that none should perish, and the salvation offered to us through Jesus Christ is a gift. He does not force His will upon us, but continues to woo our hearts with His unfailing love. He extends the nail-scarred hands of grace and mercy to each of us," she says. "When my heart is pierced with that double-edged sword, I am reminded that there is a time to let go. I stand on the promise that no one loves my daughters more than Jesus does."

Nancy Williams is a licensed professional counselor and the author of *Secrets to Parenting Your Adult Child*,[1] so I asked her for her thoughts on this all-important issue: How can we be more like Jochebed? What are some steps we can take as moms to trusting, relinquishing, and ultimately surrendering our children to the Lord? Her answer was poignant . . . and powerful:

> As both a parent and a mental health professional, I've learned that letting go—in exciting times as well as heartbreaking circumstances—is a challenging process that takes understanding, patience, courage, and time. We must work through our

---

1. Nancy Williams, *Secrets to Parenting Your Adult Child* (Bloomington, MN: Bethany House, 2011).

own grief, concerns, hesitancies, perhaps even fears, as we help others adjust to the changes that may come. Most importantly, we must relinquish our sense of control, and trust that God loves the one we love even more than we do. And He is right there to guide, to comfort, to heal, and to love. He never lets go.[2]

What a comfort! The God who molded the galaxies . . . who keeps the planet turning at just the right speed, the perfect distance from the sun—this God, who created the world and all that it holds, holds us as well. His strong arms surround us, even when we can't feel them.

My oldest child was quite hyperactive, and when he was a baby, I sometimes had to literally restrain him in my arms to get him to go to sleep. As bedtime approached, I held Jordan in the rocking chair, singing softly and rocking him, with my arms holding him so that he couldn't squirm away. He cried in fatigue and frustration a bit, but he would ultimately succumb to the Sandman. Most nights, even after he fell asleep, I held him for a while, breathing in his scent—a mix of baby shampoo, formula, and sweat.

Even (especially!) when I'm fighting Him, God holds my heart and spirit until I let myself be quieted by His love. Zephaniah 3:17 says, "The LORD your God is with you, the Mighty Warrior who saves. He will take great delight in you; in his love he will no longer rebuke you, but will rejoice over you with singing."

And dear one, He *will* hold us even if we have to experience the hardest thing a mother could ever face.

His Extraordinary Tapestry

Jan Riddlespurger, a wife and mom I've known since I was a little girl, has that kind of story. I want you to hear from her, in her own words:

---

2. Personal email communication with author Dena Dyer, December 27, 2011.

I first became a mom on April 14, 1978. (Remember that date, as God was already up to something.) He gave me a beautiful little girl, whom we named Leslie. She loved life, singing, dancing, and playing the piano. She sped through life. Her brother, Bryan, joined us three years after she did, completing my dream of a family. The moments flew by, and I joined the ranks of parents with grown children, who would love to be able to replay each moment, slowly now. Every. Single. One.

Back on Thanksgiving Day, 1990, my husband, Dave, made the hardest diagnosis of his professional life. Leslie had recently been released from the hospital with no answers, after undergoing many tests to determine the cause of extreme headaches and nausea. Dave took his ophthalmoscope and discovered papilledema, which was a result of swelling in the brain, pushing on the optic nerve.

His expression told me he now knew what the physicians had been missing for nearly two months. Further tests revealed that our beautiful daughter had a malignant medulloblastoma—a brain tumor.

For the next year and a half, she experienced two brain surgeries, radiation and chemo, and then the cancer began to spread through her spinal column.

In the midst of this horrible illness, Leslie would pick up prayer cards at church to pray for others. She was genuinely concerned about her friends' eternal choices. (I knew she had settled the question about her own eternity with Jesus sometime before her illness began.)

And in my faltering moments, the Lord was faithful to remind me that she was His child, and He loved her far more than I ever could. Selfishly, I wanted to keep her here with me. But after only fourteen short years, a total of 5,138 days, the Lord called her to come home to Him.

The pain of letting her go was unimaginable. She was my little girl! But I want you to know that God counted my every single tear and heartache, and blessed me with a huge measure of grace, even in my deepest sorrow.

Fast forward many years later and I was asked to mentor a young woman. I was busy, and almost said no. But God impressed on me that I should say yes. Little did I know, He was up to something amazing.

Our mentoring ministry is set up so that the mentors and mentees are matched by a prayerful team of women. Though the team knew nothing of my story as the mom of a cancer victim, they matched me with Sandra. She had a young daughter with a malignant brain tumor, and the prognosis looked pretty grim.

We met at a kick-off event, excitedly exchanged hugs, and then we exchanged basic information: family names, phone numbers, addresses, and our birthdates. As I wrote Sandra's birthdate, April 14, 1972, I could hardly see through the tears.

She was incredulous as I told her that my daughter, Leslie, was born on her sixth birthday. I explained about Leslie's illness, and discovered that her daughter, Kelsey, also had a medulloblastoma. What an extraordinary tapestry the Lord weaves!

Sandra and I met every week for the next two years. She came to know the Lord as her Savior, as did her husband and her eldest daughter, with Lisa giving her testimony before our entire congregation. Kelsey was the most loving little girl imaginable. And Sandra transformed right before my eyes, finding the extraordinary grace and mercy the Lord gives to those who reside in His arms.

After a long, hard fight with her terrible illness, Kelsey now knows His love face-to-face. In turn, Sandra has been a strong friend for others who have experienced such deep grief.

I can honestly say that although I would have never chosen most of this road I have traveled, I would not change it.

I would not change it. How many of us could say those words after traveling through the pain and agony of losing a child? You see, Jan found something in common with God. He lost a child too. He knows how we feel! We can cry on His shoulder, expressing deep hurt, anger, sadness, and grief over our loss. It's unbelievable but true: Christ can become our dearest friend.

When we suffer, He cries. Isaiah 63:9–10 says, "In all their distress he too was distressed, and the angel of his presence saved them. In his love and mercy he redeemed them; he lifted them up and carried them all the days of old."

No matter how difficult it is to release a child (whether through death like Jan, through their willful choices like Connie, or from just growing older), may our prayer be to look for wisdom and understanding in all things. Proverbs 2:4–5 says, "If you look for it as for silver and search for it as for hidden treasure, then you will understand the fear of the Lord and find the knowledge of God."

God's knowledge is far greater than ours. He is able to take a heart-wrenching situation—such as Jochebed having to release Moses into another woman's care—and turn it into a glory far greater than we could imagine. He used every part of Moses's life to prepare him for greatness.

Beloved, we might not understand everything that God asks us to endure. Some days, we may feel as if our hearts will never mend. However, we can rest assured that He will be with us through it all. When we are short on faith, or lack the desire to even pray, we can ask others to hold us up in prayer. We can pray (as I have, many times): "Lord, give me the desire to desire You." And we can look forward to heaven, where we will never have to let go of the ones we love.

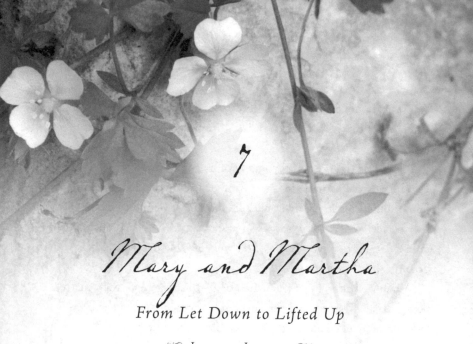

7

Mary and Martha

From Let Down to Lifted Up

❧ Luke 10; John 11 ❧

TINA ❧ "Sing a new song to the LORD! . . . Publish his glorious deeds" (Ps. 96:1, 3 NLT). My heart enthused at the thought. Friends and family members urged me to record a CD of my original music, and after seeking the Lord about it, I took this Scripture as confirmation. After deciding to move forward, I chose to presell the CDs to raise money for the project. I raised all but the last one thousand dollars.

I know that to some, a thousand dollars is like pennies, but for a small, struggling pastor's family, it felt overwhelming. I waited, prayed, and tried more presales. Nothing happened. The river stopped flowing, the funds ran dry, and I became desperate. In my own futile attempt to fix it, I fumbled through my directory to find someone to call for the loan. I felt defeated in expectation and hope. Months passed and I could have saved the money by then; instead, I continued to wallow in the hurt. I felt God had abandoned me. In my deepest desperation, I cried out to God, "Where are You? Why aren't You helping?"

What happens when we feel disappointed, defeated, or wounded by

God? Is it okay to confess such an emotion? As I write, memories of painful disappointing moments flood my thoughts. I recall shocking outbursts stemming from dashed hopes, and excessive dissatisfaction with people—and God. Dare I confess that?

"Defeated in expectation or hope"—that is how Merriam-Webster defines *disappointed*. We have all worn the letter *D* at the center of our attire. Some wear it bitterly, while others guiltily try to hide it. Either way, it's a wound many of us face.

Wounded in Expectation

Two sisters, Martha and Mary, lived in a small village named Bethany. Today, Bethany lies two miles southeast of Jerusalem. Martha opened her home to Jesus, and He probably stopped by every time He and His disciples traveled through. There, Jesus found food and rest. I picture it as a beautiful place, because Martha had the gift of hospitality.

On one particular day, Martha scurried around to prepare the meal while Jesus rested and shared His stories. While working, Martha noticed Mary sitting at the feet of Jesus, rather than helping with the meal. Men often gathered for teaching, but most of the time women were not permitted in those circles. As Martha diligently served, her heart rate increased. She expected Mary to tend to her role, not only as a host, but as a woman. Suddenly fed up, she complained to Jesus, "Lord, don't you care that my sister has left me to do the work by myself? Tell her to help me!" (Luke 10:40). Though her complaint seemed legitimate, Jesus felt differently: "'Martha, Martha,' the Lord answered, 'you are worried and upset about many things, but few things are needed—or indeed only one. Mary has chosen what is better, and it will not be taken away from her'" (vv. 41– 42).

Let's read it again: "Mary has chosen what is better, and it will not be taken away from her."

What a blow to a servant's heart! Did Martha say to herself, "But, Jesus, don't you see what I am doing for you? Isn't it good as well?" Was her spirit crushed because her efforts weren't recognized as she expected? Did she feel disappointed in expectation? Of course. Wouldn't many of us feel wounded in this way? However, Jesus didn't set out to hurt Martha's feelings. He wanted to set her free.

In Joanna Weaver's book *Lazarus Awakening,* she shares that Jesus offered Martha freedom: "Freedom from the God she thought He was, forever demanding more, always more, and a higher quality, always higher. In Christ she found a God who wanted to share life, not consume it. A Father who wanted her love more than He wanted her busy service."[1]

There are times when we expect Jesus and others to respond a certain way. Martha expected Jesus to rebuke Mary for her outrageous behavior; He did not. In fact, He affirmed it. When we feel God has spanked our hands or put us in our place, it stings. Our expectations of Him are shattered.

That would not be the only time Jesus let Martha down. There was yet a greater, more pressing and urgent moment, far more important than preparing a meal; a moment of life and death.

Wounded in Hope

Mary and Martha's brother, Lazarus, became ill. At some point, they faced a realization that his sickness had progressed to the point of death. In the midst of that shocking revelation, they hurried someone out the door to find Jesus and deliver the message, "Lord, the one you love is sick" (John 11:3). In essence, they were saying: "Hurry! Come quickly! He needs you!"

A few years ago, I journeyed home at an unplanned time. The morning after my arrival, I checked on my mom and found her vomiting in the bathroom. As we walked to her room, she leaned against me and I

---

1. Joanna Weaver, *Lazarus Awakening* (Colorado Springs: WaterBrook Press, 2012), 41.

felt her illness. My concern intensified when I helped her into bed. In an instant, her head fell to one side while her eyes rolled to the other. I clutched her limp head in my hands and called her name. No response. I checked for breathing; thankfully, she was still taking in air. Stricken with fear and panic, I shouted for my niece to call 911. I urgently shared the emergency with the operator. "The ambulance is on its way," she assured me.

When the sisters sent word to Jesus, letting him know how sick their brother had become, it was their way of calling 911. Their hope was similar to what we want from a 911 call. We expect responders to hurry. But Jesus did not.

> When he heard this, Jesus said, "This sickness will not end in death. No, it is for God's glory. . . ." He stayed where he was two more days, and then he said to his disciples, "Let us go back to Judea." (vv. 4–7)

Imagine the whirl of emotions you'd experience if in the midst of an emergency, you dialed 911, and the ambulance never showed up. How many times have we shouted, "Help me, Jesus!" and then felt as if He never came?

Jesus waited two days before leaving Jerusalem. "Bethany was less than two miles from Jerusalem" (v. 18). Jesus understood the distance and time it would take to travel to a town he frequently visited. Not only did He understand, but Mary and Martha understood the distance and time as well. Jesus waited two days before leaving and then took two days to travel. He was certainly in no hurry.

Some scholars believe the wait may have been due to the Jewish belief that the soul hovers over the body for three days. Perhaps Jesus waited so the people would be sure that Lazarus was truly dead. But Jesus gave us a more passionate reason for waiting in verse 4, "This sickness will not end in death. No, it is for God's glory."

The wait didn't mean rejection—it meant the end result would be far greater than any healing Mary and Martha could imagine. "On his arrival, Jesus found that Lazarus had already been in the tomb for four days. . . . When Martha heard that Jesus was coming, she went out to meet him, but Mary stayed at home. 'Lord,' Martha said to Jesus, 'if you had been here, my brother would not have died'" (vv. 17, 20–21).

Do those words resonate with us? Of course they do—I've said them myself. "If you had only done such-and-such, this situation wouldn't have happened."

Years ago, my husband wanted to invite a certain man—we will call him "Bob"—into his trusted circle. The Lord helped me discern specific things regarding Bob; therefore, I didn't trust him. I shared my concerns with my husband, but ultimately he needed to pray through it. Eventually, he decided to invite Bob into his life. Almost a year later, Bob betrayed my husband's confidence. He created a huge uproar that ended in pain and suffering for our entire family. I remember saying to my husband, "If you had only followed my advice, this wouldn't have happened."

I became a "Martha." In my puddle of pain, God reminded me that this situation wasn't a mess. God could and did use those events to teach, reveal, and heal our family. But in that moment, I would have never thought it possible. Sometimes our lack of understanding of what God might be trying to do can keep us from seeing the big picture.

Mary was so hurt by Jesus's late arrival that she couldn't even come out and face him. Now that's disappointment! It's easy to lose confidence in God when we feel wounded in such a way.

Death to Life

Martha stepped forward to face Jesus. Can't we imagine the tension between them?

Jesus said to her, "Your brother will rise again."

Martha answered, "I know he will rise again in the resurrection at the last day."

Jesus said to her, "I am the resurrection and the life. The one who believes in me will live, even though they die; and whoever lives by believing in me will never die. Do you believe this?" (vv. 23–26)

Though Martha said yes, she didn't get it. Martha knew Jesus as the healer, but she had no concept that He could actually raise someone from the dead—or did she? Had rumors spread of His healing the widow's son from Nain? Though strict orders were given to tell no one of His healing Jairus's daughter, had word of it reached Bethany? If she indeed held knowledge of those miracles, then the wound of Jesus waiting must have felt more excruciating and confusing.

Martha didn't understand what Jesus was trying to say. When we are thirsty, He is water; when we are hungry, He is bread; when we are dying, He is life. He is all we need. Her call for Jesus was to have Him heal Lazarus before his death, but Jesus needed Martha and Mary to experience something far greater.

Jesus asked Martha to go and get Mary. Upon her arrival, she voiced the same words as Martha.

When Jesus saw her weeping,. . . he was deeply moved in spirit and troubled. "Where have you laid him?" he asked.

"Come and see, Lord," they replied.

Jesus wept. (vv. 33–35)

It grieved Jesus to see Mary and Martha disappointed in Him. It grieved Him equally that the people didn't believe. That is the wound Jesus carried.

This moment, when Jesus wept, has raised questions and eyebrows. We know our responses when we're disappointed, but is it possible Jesus could be moved emotionally by our behavior? The Greek word for "deeply moved" is *embrimaomai*, meaning "to snort with anger, to have indignation on, straightly charge, groan, or murmur against." Though Jesus was all deity, He was also all man. Jesus had no reason to cry for Lazarus. He knew Lazarus was about to be raised from the dead. His concern wasn't with the dead but the living. So we can resolve, Jesus's emotion wasn't just about losing a friend.

When Jesus saw the tears from Mary and the people, He was "deeply moved in spirit *and* troubled." What was Jesus really troubled about? That they blamed Him for Lazarus's death, that the people did not believe? Or was it because of their tears? The Greek word for "troubled" is *tarassō* meaning "to stir or agitate." It's the same word used when King Herod heard that a new king had been born. He was "troubled." He was "agitated." Can we safely say Jesus may have been "agitated" by the people's unbelief? The tears of the people were not only the result of their loss, but because of how they felt, as evident from their first expressions: "Couldn't he have kept this man from dying?" The tears expressed their grief . . . and their disappointment.

Perhaps the tears from Jesus came from his compassion for their mourning, as well as the emotion He felt due to their unbelief and disappointment in Him.

Still, true to His word, Jesus stood before the stench and the stone. Through His own tears, with intense emotion, He shouted, "Lazarus, come out!" (v. 43). As the wide-eyed crowd watched, Lazarus stepped out of the darkness and into the light. What an amazing moment! The Bible says that because of that miracle, many people believed in Jesus.

A Pouring Out

Time passed, and six days before the Passover, Jesus made His way back to Bethany for another dinner, this time given in His honor.

Perhaps this was a way the three could extend their thanks to Jesus for resurrecting Lazarus . . . or did they know this would be their last dinner with Him?

"Martha served, while Lazarus was among those reclining at the table with him" (John 12:2). Because I was raised with eight brothers, I get a clear picture of the guys reclining at the table. Martha poured out her love of service and hospitality; Lazarus poured out his friendship and fellowship; but where was Mary? Once again, she's not in her respected place or tending to her duties. Mary's thoughts and heart lay elsewhere.

The chatter and rattle of preparations continued while Mary, moved with emotion, rose and came to the table to deliver a touching and dramatic display. She "took about a pint of pure nard, an expensive perfume; she poured it on Jesus's feet and wiped his feet with her hair" (v. 3).

To fall at the feet of someone and pour an entire bottle of expensive perfume on them must have seemed foolish and irrational! I'm sure the disciples jumped up, Martha stopped working, and everyone gawked. But Mary didn't care. A gut-wrenching sensation swelled within her, and she buried her head at the base of His legs. Imagine tears falling on His calloused feet, mixing with the flow of the liquid. Strands of her hair lay to the side, until she gently took them and swabbed the top of His feet.

An awkward silence filled the air . . . as beautiful fragrance slowly drifted upward.

Earlier, Mary couldn't even face Jesus. Earlier, she said, "If you had only come sooner . . ." Earlier, her heart was crushed, broken, and disappointed in Jesus. What happened after Jesus raised Lazarus from the dead? Was there time to clear the thick tension that occurred between Jesus and His dear friends? How many times have we kept our distance and love from someone because of our disappointment?

Mary found an altar; not a glorious one, or one where she had to stack stones. Instead, it was an altar she could fall upon right where she stood, spilling out not only her most prized possession, but also every emotion within her. To physically touch the feet of Jesus . . . that is something we all look forward to doing.

Hearing a pastor speak on this subject, something struck me. What if this beautiful act was Mary's way of saying, "I'm sorry"? What if this was her way of asking Jesus to forgive her? Was she confessing, "Oh, Lord, I *do* believe"? I believe that as she poured out the perfume, she was pouring out her love, and also pouring out her hurt and disappointment—letting it go and laying it down.

I have found myself on the floor in such a place, agony stricken and filled with a desire to pour out my repentance to God for my unbelief. I had messed up; I hadn't waited; I didn't trust. I needed to pour out my admiration for Him, for who He is and will forevermore be. To cry out, "That really hurt, but I still love you!" Could this moment between Mary and Jesus have been something more than what we've always heard?

Martha and Mary felt wounded by Jesus. Martha went out to meet with Jesus, ready to face Him, speak to Him, and confront Him. She didn't go in pretense; she didn't try to shove everything under the rug as if she were okay. She came in honesty and conviction. In this poignant act, Mary also came to the Lord, but in her own way, broken and spilled out, humbled, without words. Yet, her heart spoke loudly. We too can come to Jesus like Martha and Mary. Nothing can stop us; nothing can stand in our way. At the idea of anyone trying, Jesus Himself will rise and declare, "Leave her alone!"

And He will breathe us in, like the warmth of the sun. He will receive us, just as He did Mary and Martha. He will declare life to come forward, as He did with Lazarus. And in His embrace, all His words will ring true.

Almost one year after it began, I felt I had finally surrendered the CD project to God, but had I really? My hurt and disappointment in God still lingered. One evening, I received a call from a woman who sometimes attended our church. Before her call, I hadn't seen her in a while.

She asked to visit me. I said yes; it wasn't unusual for someone to come for counseling or prayer. After answering the door, I immediately heard, "I have something for you."

I opened the white envelope she handed me and pulled out a check for one thousand dollars. I stood speechless, my emotions bubbling. I'll never forget her words: "I would have brought it sooner, but I was waiting for it to get here."

After saying good-bye, I looked down at the check and God's revealed plan. There was a reason for the wait I had endured! I thanked Him for using this wonderful woman, for the blessing of her generosity, and for stopping me when I tried to push forward on my own. I stood in the midst of a miracle. After falling on my face and asking God to forgive me, my brokenness and unbelief dissolved.

Today, God still reminds me of what Jesus said to Mary and Martha after raising Lazarus from the grave, "Did I not tell you that if you believe, you will see the glory of God?" (11:40).

DENA ❧ In what area of your life are you disappointed? Finances, health, relationships, career? Do you wonder if God is paying attention?

Oh, friend, I've been there.

So has Sheila Lagrand.

Betrayed by Her Body

Her struggle with disappointment—and ultimately anger with her Maker—started with a tonsillectomy gone wrong. That surgery featured an extended hospital stay, ice cream deprivation, and a gauze pack down her throat. She also suffered from "chicken pox that sprouted overnight like mold on stale bread. Dr. Martin told my mother it was the worst case he'd ever seen."

By the time she was five, Sheila had learned not to trust her body;

she grew "pudgy and bookish." Sheila came to see her body as a shoddy container.

At age twelve, she grew eight inches in three months. Says Sheila, "The chubby girl hiding in the library during recess morphed into a tall, gawky teen. My PE teacher said, 'With your height, you'd have a great stride. Ever think of running?' I was stunned. No one had ever encouraged me to do something physical. So each morning at half-light, I'd lace my sneakers and slip out the door. I raced past houses lit by one beacon at the kitchen window, illuminating a chortling percolator. My feet pounded the sidewalk, punishing it for my frail childhood. I'd pray as I ran: 'Father, thank You for fixing me. Thank You for making me *fast*.'"

But as Sheila was playing soccer one day, she heard a snap and pain blazed in her leg. She'd torn ligaments in her knee. Four months later, the ligaments gave way again while she danced. Six months after that, they tore as she climbed from the back seat of a two-door car. "No more running," the orthopedist told her. "This knee can't take it. We'll repair it when you're done growing, but you need to avoid stressing that joint."

Sheila responded by crying angry tears. She prayed, "God, they say You don't make junk. Why did You trap me in this rusty bucket?" At eighteen, she submitted to reconstructive surgery, but at her final postoperative appointment, the doctor told her not to resume running. Sheila was crushed: "My body was a dungeon, and the door had slammed shut. I ran in my sleep and awoke crying."

Sheila's disappointment with the way God made her body resonated with me. At twenty-four years old, while traveling with a singing group, I became seriously ill. A severe, unrelenting fatigue progressed into strep throat and ultimately mononucleosis. Mono forced me to leave the group and recuperate for several weeks at my childhood home. I never fully recovered—and almost twenty years later, I continue to deal (some days more than others) with chronic fatigue, depression, and other symptoms of autoimmune disease. In addition, a car wreck in college resulted in back and neck issues that still bother me.

My Own Admission

At times, I feel okay. I realize that I'm extremely blessed and have much to be grateful for. At other times, I succumb to the temptation to dwell on my physical problems and throw a full-blown pity party (complete with decorations). I alternate between angrily confronting God with my questions, like Martha, and sulking in a corner, refusing to talk to Him—like Mary.

As I'm writing this chapter, I've spent the last several months suffering with headaches. Some of them have been severe. Lately, they've been unrelenting. Talk about discouraging! I recently had an MRI, and will have to undergo more testing to determine the cause of the headaches. The radiologist said my brain wasn't normal for someone my age. I don't want to be "special" in that way, believe me!

On the hardest days, when everything hurts—including my bank account—I list my laments: My patient husband has too often picked up my slack. I haven't always been able to fully participate in my family members' and friends' lives. My kids don't really know what it's like to have a consistently energetic, healthy mom. And I've sometimes had to turn down writing, speaking, and singing opportunities because of frail health.

See? I'm good at self-pity. I've cried oceans of tears in frustration and asked God to mend my broken body so many times that I've lost count. I wholeheartedly believe He could heal my worn-out frame with a word—and yet He doesn't. Why?

There are no easy answers.

However, what I have found, in the midst of my day-to-day life, is that He gives me spiritual strength when I humble myself and ask for it. When I repent of self-pity, confess my frustration, and turn to Scripture instead of to the world's numbing agents (television, magazines) or sinful habits (gossiping, arguing, and complaining), He leads me to the perfect encouraging word for my specific situation.

Journaling is another helpful tool I've found to keep depression at bay. Each day, I try to list specific blessings, from small (a white butterfly in my flower bed) to large (an unexpected check in the mail which covers a medical expense) in a journal. This simple practice has often gotten me back on track in the midst of trying times.

In addition, God has led me to doctors, diets, supplements, and medicines that help me make the most of what I've been given. When I eat more plant-based foods, I feel better. Exercise helps, as does sunlight. A sleep study found I had mild sleep apnea, and getting deeper rest gives me much better coping skills. While there isn't a cure for autoimmune disease (yet), there are things I can do to improve my quality of life. They take discipline, but they are worth it.

Go Ye, Therefore and—What?

Sometimes our disappointment with God stems from a lack of career direction or opportunities, or a confusion about the ways God is leading. Linda Thomas and her husband, Dave, worked with Wycliffe Bible Translators for three years in South America and eight years in Africa. As a teen, Linda had studied journalism and creative writing. After college, she took writing courses and workshops and published freelance articles. She said, "I'd always longed for a job that involved writing." So when Wycliffe granted her a journalism position, she was surprised when disappointed tears came to her eyes.

And then she realized why she was crying: "Compared to my previous ministries, journalism seemed insignificant—trivial, marginal. For five years, I had taught Bible classes. I'd spent all day and almost every evening, even weekends, studying the Bible and preparing lessons. I worked on the front lines of Christianity—*or so I thought*—and could find nothing in the Bible that says, 'Go ye, therefore, and work as a journalist.'"

Linda went through a period of depression. "For a year and a half, I grieved my loss of meaningful ministry. In Nairobi, Kenya, I no longer leaped out of bed in the mornings, eager to get to work. Deflated, I trudged mechanically on irrelevant fringes of real ministry."

Then one day, she came upon Psalm 96:3 (NLT). She had read it many times before, but that day it took on new meaning. "It tells us to publish God's amazing deeds and tell everyone about the wondrous things He does," she said. That verse led Linda to Psalm 9:11: "Proclaim . . . what he has done." Then she stumbled upon Psalm 105:1 and Isaiah 12:5, which tell believers to declare God's greatness and let others know what God has done.

Patiently and gently, God had led her to the truth: no job is more "holy" than another. He could use—and bless—every single gift and career. She realized that her calling "was not about writing articles and making videos! No, it was about telling others the amazing things God does in people's lives once they have Scriptures in their own languages."

The message of Wycliffe's magazines and videos is, "Look what God has done!" God lit up those verses for Linda so that she finally understood: "Words are among God's most powerful and effective tools. What would our lives be like if we did not have God's written Word? I can't fathom it, can you? Imagine how impoverished we would be if ordinary people had not used words to encourage, teach, admonish, guide, reconcile, and heal us!"

After Linda found those Bible verses, she grieved no more. Instead, she jumped out of bed each morning, on fire. She felt both humbled and honored to fill a journalism role for God, and worked with passion: "God granted me the privilege of using words to tell what He was doing across Africa—one person at a time, one family at a time, one church at a time, one community at a time."[2]

Freedom in the Midst of Trials

What unrelenting, surprising, or confusing situation in your own life has caused you to question God?

---

2. Adapted from Linda K. Thomas, *Grandma's Letters from Africa* (Bloomington, IN: iUniverse, 2010). Linda blogs at http://www.grandmaslettersfromafrica .blogspot.com. Used with permission.

Perhaps, like Sheila and me, your body is weak and you along with your doctors have done everything possible. You've prayed, cried, confessed, and changed your unhealthy habits. Still, you suffer. *Is God even listening?* you wonder.

Maybe you believe God has called you to minister, but no doors have opened. Or, like Linda, the doors that have opened aren't the ones you expected or desired. Still, you study and pray. *Did I hear Him right?* you ask.

Have you experienced the death of a loved one, just as Martha and Mary did with Lazarus? And when you're honest with yourself, do you wonder why God didn't step in? Losing someone dear to us often provokes a crisis of faith. After all, if God is the God we believe in, we reason, why doesn't He always come through? Why does He heal some people—and not others?

When our prayers seem to bounce off the ceiling and back into our face, what should we do? Is shaking our fist at God an appropriate response?

Jesus is our example in this, as in all things. When He was on the cross, dying a cruel death by the hands of His enemies, He shouted at God, wondering why His Father had (seemingly) abandoned Him.

Obviously, Jesus felt abandoned and alone. However, with the power at His disposal, He could have freed Himself and destroyed the people tormenting Him. Instead, He continued to submit to the will of His Father. Our Savior knew that the only way for us to receive a right relationship with God was for Him to die. Like Lazarus's death, Jesus's crucifixion served a purpose in God's redemptive plan.

The miraculous resurrection would come later. Jesus longed for Martha and Mary to receive something more than a miracle, and He wants the same for us. He wants us to find freedom—not just from our problems, but in the *midst* of our problems.

Dear sisters, life is tough. Circumstances and people will repeatedly disappoint us. But our loving heavenly Father will only transform discouraging, difficult, and draining circumstances into growth if we *allow* Him to.

The cross is the ultimate symbol of such a transformation. Jesus Himself bowed His will to the Father, submitting to humiliation and death in order that we might have access to God Almighty. And when the suffering was over, Christ exchanged a crown of thorns for a throne and jewels.

Likewise, when we offer up our sorrows to Jesus, He takes the raw material of our hurt and sculpts it into something exquisite: "Not only so, but we also glory in our sufferings, because we know that suffering produces perseverance; perseverance, character; and character, hope. And hope does not put us to shame, because God's love has been poured out into our hearts through the Holy Spirit, who has been given to us" (Rom. 5:3–5).

Then, when we have exchanged grief for hope, we are able to comfort others with that same hope (see 2 Cor. 1:4). I have seen this principle at work in my own life. Not only has God allowed me to encourage others with the comfort He has given me, but also God has used my physical limitations to bring about a desperation for His presence and power.

I can't remember a time when I felt "good" before a speaking engagement, but the very thing that frustrates me is the tool that God uses to remind me to rely on Him. Before talking to a group, I always utter these words I once heard from Beth Moore: "Lord, show up, or I'm toast!"

And He always does.

Remember Sheila, whose story we visited earlier in the chapter? Sheila's body wasn't as strong as she would have liked. After she married, pregnancy filled her with trepidation. She miscarried twice and during her third pregnancy, she was hospitalized with preterm labor. Sheila *begged* God to give her a healthy baby.

When God answered yes to that particular prayer, her years of anger melted away. This time, her unreliable body—which had so often felt like a prison—hadn't let her down. "He blessed me with an exquisite, full-term baby girl. As she took her first breath, my husband cried. I laughed from sheer joy," she related. "A nurse lay her in my exhausted arms. As I held her, marveling at her long eyelashes, I felt years of resentment leave my heart, crowded out by peace. God's mercy made me a mother; His grace wiped away a lifetime of tears. As I clutched my baby, my heart knelt and gave thanks."

Isn't that a great end to her story? Sometimes, as He did with Lazarus's resurrection, God surprises us with joy. At other times, He lingers and causes us to wait in silence and confusion. But He always gives us His presence, even when He withholds the presents.

He longs for us to turn *to* Him, and not away from Him, in the midst of our disappointments. When we can learn such a life-altering habit, we've found a great treasure.

This I know for sure: even when life doesn't turn out the way I want it to, I long to know more of Christ, and who He can be in and through me. I pray that my days become less about me and more about Him— even though it means my plans and expectations will be thwarted more times than I'd like. And as I hold on to Jesus, I also hold on to the hope He gives me, because I know that this frail and troubled frame of mine will one day be fully healed.

As Philip Yancey wrote, "The Bible never belittles human disappointment . . . but it does add one key word: temporary. What we feel now, we will not always feel. Our disappointment is itself a sign, an aching, a hunger for something better. And faith is, in the end, a kind of homesickness—for a home we have never visited but have never once stopped longing for."[3]

Paul says, "Therefore we do not lose heart. Though outwardly we are wasting away, yet inwardly we are being renewed day by day. For our light and momentary troubles are achieving for us an eternal glory that

---

3. Philip Yancey, *Disappointment with God* (Grand Rapids: Zondervan, 1988), 276.

far outweighs them all. So we fix our eyes not on what is seen, but on what is unseen, since what is seen is temporary, but what is unseen is eternal" (2 Cor. 4:16–18). Such a glorious promise makes me want to bow at His feet, like Mary did, and pour out the rest of my days as a fragrant sacrifice. It compels me to pray for holiness, that I might minister hope out of the comfort He's given me.

Won't you join me?

8

Wounded Relationships

From Passion to Pain

❧ Gen. 3; 1 Kings 16, 19, 21; Hosea; 2 Sam. 11, 12 ❧

TINA ❧ Chaos broke out. Screams and shouts resounded through the entire house. The fighting drove them to the back yard. One raced here and the other there, still raising their voices at one another. My parents continued to fight stronger, louder, and with greater intensity. This fight was worse than any in a long while.

As hostility raced, clouds gathered overhead and rumbled with them. In the heated moment, my father clenched his fist and hit the tall Texas pine next to him. My mother prayed silently: "Lord, help me to know what to do." And just as their anger rose to its highest level, something unimaginable happened.

A bolt of lightning struck the tree that stood between my parents. Bark flew from its side and hit my father in the head. Smoke drifted upward as the two jumped in fear and confusion. With deafened ears, they closed their mouths, walked inside, and remained married for fifty-two years.

Someone once said, "Marriage is a three-ring circus: engagement ring, wedding ring, and suffering."[1] Sadly, suffering often attaches itself to marriages and dating relationships. I'll never forget the story that my mother and father shared with me. It was not the last time my parents fought, but it was the last time they fought with such anger and hostility. They realized God was trying to get their attention, and they were ready to listen.

The hurts stemming from marriage and dating relationships can wound us more deeply than any other. It wasn't God's plan that such wounding should take place in our relationships.

Like many women, we grew up thinking real life would turn out as it does in fairy tales: damsel meets a prince, he comes to her rescue, and they live happily ever after. However, life is definitely not a fairy tale, and the only perfect relationships are those in heaven. Even when we love someone—and that someone loves us in return—our humanness gets in the way, and deep wounds result. Four couples from Scripture—Adam and Eve, Ahab and Jezebel, Hosea and Gomer, and David and Bathsheba—wounded one another, sometimes profoundly. Let's take a look at the traps they fell into, the costs of giving in to temptation, and the losses they suffered. If nothing else, these all-too-human figures can be a cautionary tale for our contemporary relationships.

Adam and Eve: Giving in to Blame

God gave Adam and Eve a key to a beautiful garden. The place emanated grandeur and fruitfulness of every kind. No one had to pull weeds or pick stickers out of their feet. It was an amazing, sculpted piece of landscape. They could do anything they wanted—except eat the fruit from one particular tree. I imagine Adam and Eve's marriage as perfect in every way. They were pure, lovely, innocent, and without sin. But Satan entered the picture, disguised as a snake, and changed it

---

1. Proverbia, "Marriage," accessed March 27, 2013, http://en.proverbia.net/citastema.asp?tematica=736&page=3.

all. Today, Satan is still trying to nudge his way into relationships and marriages.

Eve seemed easily deceived by her desire. She lusted for a piece of fruit that would supposedly turn her into something fantastic. Satan deceived her into thinking she could be something far greater than the perfection God created.

> When the woman saw that the fruit of the tree was good for food and pleasing to the eye, and also desirable for gaining wisdom, she took some and ate it. She also gave some to her husband, who was with her, and he ate it. (Gen. 3:6)

After she chose to cross a boundary, unlock a door she should have kept sacred, and step into sin, life was never the same. From that moment on, hardship awaited Eve and her family.

Does the first part of the Scripture sound familiar? What fruit has the enemy enticed you into believing is good for you? That symbol of "fruit" continues to destroy marriages.

The truth is that men and women today are facing crises in their marriages. We have become a country where getting a divorce is the norm, even in the church. It's far too easy to dismiss one partner and grab another one . . . and battling for our marriages seems too difficult. How I admire those who have worked diligently to restore their marriages! But if one person in the relationship is willing to be reconciled and move toward healing, and the other is not, the willing spouse can feel overwhelming despair.

Adam blamed Eve and God for his actions, while Eve blamed the serpent for hers. No one was willing to take full responsibility for what happened. Eve was, indeed, at fault and responsible for her actions, but Adam was also wrong, and he bore responsibility too.

In the midst of arguments, disappointments, and misunderstandings, we often blame others instead of taking responsibility. I wonder how Eve felt when her husband was asked by God, "Have you eaten from the tree that I commanded you not to eat from?" and he answered, "The woman you put here with me—she gave me some fruit from the tree, and I ate it" (Gen. 3:11–12). Adam wasn't lying, but he didn't own up to his part, either.

Tom Pals—a friend, counselor, and pastor—says, "What must that have been like, for Eve to listen to her husband not only shift the responsibility for his choice to her, but to God Himself? When Adam said, 'The woman you put here with me . . . ,' he was blaming God for his decision to sin! In effect, Adam is telling God, 'You know, God, if you hadn't created her and put her in this paradise with me, none of this would have happened.' Listening to Adam, Eve follows his lead, but softens the accusation and says, 'The serpent deceived me. . . .' In effect, Eve is saying, 'I was lied to. How can you hold me responsible when it was the serpent you put here that led me astray?'"

You see, love does not dishonor (shame, disgrace) others, it is not self-seeking, and it always protects (see 1 Cor. 13:4–7). Adam didn't need to lie in order to share those qualities with Eve. He could have been honest with God and respected his wife at the same time. Adam could have, as Tom says, said, "'Yes, I ate from the tree,' and let that simple truth stand as a confession of his sin. But he didn't."

The wounding Eve experienced from her husband is something we can relate to. We wound when we blame.

Ahab and Jezebel: Giving in to Negative Influences

Along with blaming, we can also feed off each other's negative behaviors, which often results in wounding. Ahab and Jezebel's dysfunctional relationship hurt not only themselves, but others along the way.

Jezebel, a dominant and powerful woman, served the god Baal and the fertility goddess Ashtoreth. Ahab did more evil in the eyes of the Lord than any other king who came before him. He also married

Jezebel, and began to serve and worship Baal (1 Kings 16:30–31). This passage gives us a clue into how our mate's negative behaviors can influence our own. From the beginning, their relationship was not grounded in the One True God. When my mother met my father, she was a devout Christian woman and he was a loose cannon. After three months of dating, they eloped. Her decision to marry a man who wasn't grounded in the same faith wreaked havoc on their marriage. Early on in their marriage, she allowed my father's actions to influence her in a negative way. Thank goodness, she never strayed too far from the cross. And they remained married for fifty-two years.

Ahab and Jezebel were both evil people who fed off each other's sinful behavior. After Elijah had the prophets of Jezebel murdered, Ahab rushed home to tattle, which spurred Jezebel's fury to kill Elijah.

After finding Ahab in a pit of pity for coveting Naboth's vineyard, Jezebel had Naboth stoned to death, just so Ahab could obtain the vineyard (1 Kings 21). Again, we see Ahab's behavior negatively influencing Jezebel. Of course, Jezebel is responsible for her own actions; however, she fed off his unhealthy behavior. It's not so different from what happens in relationships today.

Consider this profound statement in 1 Kings 21:25: "There was never anyone like Ahab, who sold himself to do evil in the eyes of the LORD, urged on by Jezebel his wife." How we wound each other when we allow our mate's negative behavior to cause us to sin!

The Bible says love "does not dishonor others, it is not self-seeking, it is not easily angered, it keeps no record of wrongs. Love does not delight in evil but rejoices with the truth" (1 Cor. 13:5–6). In our marriage difficulties, we must ask the Lord to reveal the truth of the situation. Let us guard our own actions so we won't negatively influence our spouse's behavior. God will reveal His truth to us, if we will yield to Him. When we hold fast to His Word, and put on the character of Christ, our actions will be pleasing to the Lord.

Hosea and Gomer—Giving in to Past Sins

The Bible doesn't give us much information about Gomer, only that she was a "promiscuous woman" (Hosea 1:2) who married a man named Hosea. God actually instructed Hosea to marry Gomer. Of course, she is used as a metaphor to show how God felt about Israel at the time. Nevertheless, I imagine the two were the talk of the town.

How much did Gomer truly value her life, if she willingly gave herself over to men? How much could Hosea value Gomer because of her past?

Gomer, though sinful in her actions, was already wounded before she ever met Hosea. She entered the relationship as a broken woman. No one knows what caused Gomer to step into that life. Was she missing a father? Was she sexually abused at a young age? Did she feel devalued and seek affirmation from men? Or was it a lifestyle she chose because she didn't know God?

Women like Gomer can sabotage their relationships because they feel they do not deserve to be happy. If you're a wounded woman with a promiscuous past and you're trying to change, know that you can turn from your sinful past and move forward with God into a glorious future. We can't fathom the depth of God's love and no one can love as deeply as Him, but if God's plan is for you to marry, He can bring an amazing, honorable man into your life (like Hosea), who will value and love you more than you ever expected. The hard part is allowing yourself to be loved, receive the blessings, and believe that you deserve them.

At some point, Gomer decided to go back to her sinful past and became pregnant with another man's baby. Deeply wounded, Hosea received her back. In the end, Gomer left once more. "The LORD said to [Hosea], 'Go, show your love to your wife again, though she is loved by another man and is an adulteress. Love her as the LORD loves the Israelites'" (Hosea 3:1).

Little did Gomer know, someone far greater than Hosea—the Almighty God—valued her life. And because God valued Gomer, He encouraged Hosea to value her, as well.

Whatever Gomer's wound, whatever caused her to run and to diminish herself, she still could not escape the love of God. Though it's easy for us to cast judgment on women like her, God understands their worth. And so He says, "Love her as the LORD loves the Israelites." Hosea paints the perfect picture of what Scripture tells us: love "always hopes, always perseveres" (1 Cor. 13:7).

David and Bathsheba—Giving in to Adultery

One night Bathsheba chose to bathe on the rooftop in clear view of King David's balcony. For some reason David couldn't sleep, rose from his bed, and found a surprise waiting for him in the moonlight.

Raymond Brown wrote in his book, *Skilful Hands: Studies in the Life of David*, "If David had gone to war he would not have seen Bathsheba that night. If she had thought seriously about her actions she would not have put temptation in his path."[2] Let's be honest—no one really knows why she chose to bathe on the roof that night. I truly feel for Bathsheba; she often gets rebuked for her part in this story. In truth, there was little she could do to stop the actions David put into motion.

Pastor Tom Pals says,

> To rebuke Bathsheba for bathing on her rooftop is to overlook whom God Himself, through His prophet Nathan, identified as the responsible party in the incident. God's characterization of Bathsheba was as "a ewe lamb" (2 Samuel 12:3) is hardly the sexually promiscuous woman that commentators have depicted. One would be hard pressed to see a ewe lamb as morally culpable for its own slaughter! God, through Nathan, said that King David "struck down Uriah the Hittite with the sword and took his wife to be (his) own." Bear in mind that

---

2. Raymond Brown, *Skilful Hands: Studies in the Life of David* (Fort Washington, PA: Christian Literature Crusade, 1972), 99.

Bathsheba was married to a non-Jew; in addition, she was the wife of a Hittite, a conquered people under Israel. She was hardly in a position to resist the summons of the King.

King David summoned Bathsheba to his quarters and the Bible says, "She came to him, and he slept with her" (2 Sam. 11:4). The sin wasn't in the look; it was in the lust. The sin wasn't the attraction; it was the action. It was in putting desire into motion, outside of God's parameters.

After David slept with Bathsheba, "she went back home" (v. 4). So many writers focus on the issue of infidelity in this story, rather than on the wound they both faced.

What emotions surged over Bathsheba once she stepped inside her home? How did she feel about what just happened? Women in the Old Testament were thought of much like property. If Bathsheba had not been married, likely no one would have thought much about her infidelity—including Bathsheba. Possibly, she would have become David's wife or part of his harem. But when the woman was married and a man took her, it was stealing. The tenth commandment makes this clear (Exod. 20:17).

Sometime after the incident with David and Bathsheba, Nathan, a prophet, came to David and shared a story with him. The tale involved a rich man who had many flocks and herds, yet stole "one little ewe lamb" from a poor man who had nourished and cared for the lamb. After hearing the story, David declared, "Surely the man who has done this deserves to die." Nathan then said to David, "You are the man!" (2 Sam. 12:5, 7).

You see, David's sin wasn't only against Bathsheba, but also her husband. David stole the lamb (Bathsheba) from Uriah. Bathsheba's wound came from being dishonored, disrespected, and used. David wounded himself because he chose to sin. Nathan opened David's eyes to see the rippling effect of his sin and the harm it brought to others. His sin resulted in the wrenching ache of being confronted—and his shattered heart over the loss of his son. Sadly, both parties were wounded because of the affair. The same wounding happens in relationships today.

Do you see yourself in this story? What are you stealing from your neighbor? In Bathsheba's case she likely had no choice, but when two people enter into a relationship, or step over a boundary because of *need* or *desire*, wounding is inevitable.

Restoration

In marriage and dating relationships, there are always two sides to every issue and every struggle. Perhaps you feel trapped in your relationship, like Bathsheba. Maybe you've stepped outside your boundaries, like David. Do you place little value on yourself, and you can relate to Gomer's wounded past? Maybe Satan has enticed you with something pleasing to the eye, like he did with Eve. In our relationships, healing takes place when the two people no longer *need* each other in an unhealthy way; instead, they individually find healing and come together as whole persons.

My husband and I both came from dysfunctional families and brought dysfunction into our marriage. Through the tough labor of working through our personal issues, our marriage has settled into a much better place. We are still learning and working on serving each other from a place of love, not neediness. The unhealthy person serves out of fear, or for the *need* of affirmation and acceptance, while the healthy person gives out of love.

Pastor Tom explains, "There are several important considerations involved in restoration. The first is dealing with unmet 'needs.' When a husband is thinking, *I need to clean the house because it will upset my wife to return and see it messy*, his perceived need is to avoid a conflict, not necessarily to do something loving for his wife. Were he to think, *I can clean the house and this will be a way of showing my wife that I love her and her peace of mind truly matters to me*, it would be a healthy desire for the betterment of their marriage. Cleaning is not the issue. The issue is what cleaning represents. To focus our energy on having someone else meet our needs is to fail to recognize the reality that God has already been meeting that need with His own loving respect and consideration for us."

Only God knows what our relationships look like and how they've wounded us. In the book *Love and Respect*, Dr. Emmerson Eggerichs writes, "In almost every case, the issue that seems to be the cause of the craziness is not the real issue at all."[3] Dr. Eggerichs would say the wife needs love and the husband needs respect. I completely agree, but what if the cause of most of our craziness is the fact that we all need more—of God?

I recently bought a plaque. On the very top, in bold letters, it reads: LOVE, and beneath that, *Love is Patient, Love is Kind*. I placed the plaque beside my desk on my windowsill. It is a great reminder to let God's love rule my actions. Interestingly, the letter "E" on the word LOVE is chipped at the very top. "How fitting," my husband said one day when he was in my office. "The letter E is broken. What a great symbol of marriage—it isn't perfect." As he left, a simple thought rushed over me: *No it isn't . . . but love is.*

Ladies, whatever you are facing in your relationships, know God can heal. Surrender your deep wounds to God. Allow Him to meet the unmet needs in your life, to change the way you view your relationships, and to reveal what steps you need to take to make the relationship everything He envisioned it to be. Have hope in the healing that awaits!

DENA ✵ My sweet mother-in-law once inscribed a card with the sentiment, "You two are proof that some marriages really are made in heaven." And while on certain days I would agree with her, on others

---

3. Emmerson Eggerichs, *Love and Respect*, (Nashville: Thomas Nelson, 2004), 31.

. . . well, let's just say that we've had disagreements that were not at all angelic.

Those fairy tales I grew up on? It didn't take long to realize that they were just stories. Carey may have been my Prince Charming, but his armor was tarnished and his horse was covered in mud. I might have been his princess, but my garb was ripped and torn.

We've now been married for sixteen wonderful years, plus a couple we don't talk about. Like any married couple, we've been through extreme highs and devastating lows. At times, one or both of us have suffered depression and doubt, and we've had days in which one or both of us wanted to leave and never come back. In some seasons, we acted like Adam and Eve, pointing our fingers at one another and blaming each other for our pain. During other hard times, we both made sinful choices and negatively influenced one another (just call us "Jezebel" and "Ahab"). We argued and yelled, sulked and pouted. It wasn't pretty, folks.

Thankfully, we've weathered the storms life has thrown at us. However, after a particularly difficult season drew to a close, I fully understood how even good marriages can end.

As I've watched several friends go through unwanted (on their end) divorces, I've also been struck by the fact that marriage vows are spoken, and broken or kept, by two separate, distinctly different people. Both spouses must be fully invested for a marriage to work. Carey and I must *both* choose daily to love each other, even when we don't feel loving.

That doesn't mean the choice is easy or fun. In fact, there are times when making a decision to love our spouse, no matter what, doesn't seem humanly possible.

And you know what? It really isn't.

Like motherhood and the ministries God has called me to, marriage has brought me to my knees more than I ever dreamed it would. But I've learned that *on my knees* is the very best place to be.

On our knees, we come to God in desperation. On our knees, we recognize our weakness. On our knees, we cry to Him, just like Peter did when he attempted to walk on water: "Help, Lord—I'm drowning!" And He always receives us there.

God has repeatedly met me at the point of my deepest need, and He wants to meet you too. Can you hear Him? He's calling, "Come to me when you are weak and weary. . . . I do not despise your weakness, My child. Actually, it draws Me closer to you, because weakness stirs up My compassion—My yearning to help. Accept yourself in your weariness, knowing that I understand how difficult your journey has been. . . . I have gifted you with fragility, providing opportunities for your spirit to blossom in My Presence."[4]

You see, God designed marriage to be a picture of Christ's love for the church. A union of two believers fully relying on Him—allowing *His* life to flow through them—is incredibly powerful. Satan doesn't like that at all. So he will throw everything in his arsenal at a godly couple to distract, distance, or even destroy them.

The hardest part of it all is that we can't control what other people do. We can only pray, make the choices God asks us to make, and set healthy boundaries. And pray some more. Hopefully, both we and our husbands will choose Jesus, joy—and our union.

My friend Katy recently shared how her marriage almost ended. Six years of money and familial stress had battered her and her husband. When their son was born, he had colic and screamed for three months, while Katy suffered from postpartum depression. A hospital job seemed an answer to their prayers; it was a big step "up" for her husband, with a good salary and benefits. But after six months, Katy's husband was laid off and was made a scapegoat for a problem he'd tried to remedy.

Katy explained, "The layoff sent him into a deep, dark hole of depression. He quit going to church and wasn't motivated to find a job.

---

4. Sarah Young, *Jesus Calling* (Nashville: Thomas Nelson, 2004), 235.

We spent all of our meager savings. I tried to work, but our two-year-old son was feeling the effects of his parents' problems and was kicked out of three different day cares. In the meantime, my spouse became so surly and said such hateful things that I was afraid he might say or do something that would make it impossible for me to forgive him."

Sadly, Katy's husband wouldn't admit he had a problem.

So Katy decided to leave. She took their son and flew to another city to stay with friends. She had no intention of ending the relationship, but she realized it would take something drastic to wake up her mate. As soon as she reached the friends' house, Katy called him.

"He sounded so despondent that when we finally hung up, I was worried he might take his own life. That night, I almost threw up while praying about it, asking God if I had pushed him over the edge rather than helping him."

But within a few days, Katy's husband contacted a counselor and asked her to come back. "I told him I would return to town but I didn't think we should live together until he had worked on the problem and made sufficient progress. So he moved in with a friend, got a part-time job, and saw the counselor twice a week—once alone and once with me. He started taking Prozac and in a short time had made great progress. We spent time together every day, rebuilding our relationship. He returned to church, and we prayed together again. After about three months we decided things had progressed enough that we could get back together, but we decided to renew our marriage vows to remake that commitment to God and to one another."

A preacher friend "remarried" the couple in his living room, with his wife and family as witnesses.

"Twenty-seven years later we're glad we didn't give up," Katy related. "By honoring our vows before God, we were able to weather the storm and build a strong and happy marriage."

I'm grateful that Katy's story had a happy ending. But what about the stories that don't?

What if a spouse strays—or leaves? What if the person you've given everything to—maybe for decades—walks out and refuses to admit their mistakes? What then?

Like Tina, I've seen women who have had this very thing happen to them. "Winnie" recently told me that her husband cheated on her, married the woman he had an affair with, and took everything: house, money, cars, and dignity. "He left me with nothing after we'd been married for twenty-five years, and I had to start over," she said. "I had to leave my dream house and go back to work—he ruined my life."

I could tell Winnie still held bitterness by the way she talked about her ex. I asked her how long ago the betrayal had happened, and was surprised by the answer: fourteen years.

Another acquaintance, "Cindy," recently shared her story in a heart-wrenching email: "My marriage is ending after twenty-four years. I'm fifty years old and alone. My husband came home one day and confessed that our whole marriage had been a lie. He had been gambling, stealing money from our son, lying about his paycheck, taking my medicine—and he had a porn addiction. Through the years of many gambling stretches, he would always say he would stop, and I would believe him. All this time, he attended church. One night, I got up in the middle of the night and found him watching porn. After he got caught, he went on a full gambling spree for four days and wouldn't return phone calls or come home. I filed for divorce, hoping it would shake him up and that he would want to save his marriage. But he wanted nothing to do with God or me."

Cindy had been faithful to her husband, helped raised two sons, and diligently worked part-time while raising a family. Now, due to her ex's sinful choices, she lost her marriage, home, health insurance, car, and credit (she had to declare bankruptcy). In addition, Cindy suffers from fibromyalgia and other health problems that keep her in constant pain.

She wrote, "All I can say is that I lived my life for God and my family, and now I'm alone. My sons fell away from the Lord and I hardly see them. I feel like everything I gave my life for has not turned out the way I hoped. I also had a group of 'Christian' friends betray me. The Lord is my hope, and I try to keep up my faith. But I find very few Christians who are there to pray and walk alongside me. This is the first time I can say I'm lonely. I miss being a wife and a mom. It's the only thing I truly with all my heart loved to do. Thanks for listening. . . . I'm grieving and waiting on the Lord to show me what to do now."

I can't pretend to understand Cindy's or Winnie's pain. I've suffered, and I've often felt lonely, even (especially) in church. But these sweet sisters-in-Christ have been asked to carry burdens far beyond what I've been forced to bear. I won't share the intimate details of the response I sent Cindy, but I do want to encourage you if you're facing a situation similar to hers or Winnie's.

Beloved one, God hasn't left. He never will. Fall on Him, and He will sustain you.

Maybe it was your choice to leave a marriage. Perhaps you committed infidelity or chose drugs, alcohol, or a career over your family. And now, the regret, shame, and loneliness are almost too much to bear. If you've been through a Bathsheba-like situation, God wants you to know that His love is the same as it's always been. No matter what you've done, or what others have done, He has not changed. And He has not—and will not!—give up on you or your loved ones.

Perhaps you say to yourself: God couldn't forgive me or restore my life. I messed up too much! Remember Hosea and Gomer. Hosea never gave up on his bride, and God will never, ever give up on you.

What about Bathsheba and David? They took part in adultery, deception, and even murder. Yet God didn't disqualify them from abundant life or—unbelievable as it is—taking part in the lineage of Christ.

If you're full of remorse over your own choices, and you don't think God's promises apply, consider Romans 3:3–4: "What if some were unfaithful? Will their unfaithfulness nullify God's faithfulness? Not at all!"

You see, God can't stop being who He is, no matter what we choose to do. He is ever-constant, ever-faithful, ever-loving.

Does He experience grief and disappointment with us? Of course. His Father-heart broke over the choices David made. Those sinful actions reverberated, resulting in tragic consequences.

Does He discipline us when we sin? Yes. Just as He did with the royal Israelite couple, He holds us accountable for our actions. He doesn't excuse our sin, but He doesn't hold it against us forever either.

Does He ever turn His back on us for good? No. Not ever. He used and blessed David and Bathsheba, not because they were perfect—but because He is. And He will use and bless you too, if you choose to follow Him.

Once, on a black day at Calvary, God seemingly turned His back on Jesus. Christ felt the coldness of His Father's absence, and He cried out, "My God, my God, why have you forsaken me?" (Matt. 27:46).

I'm sure it crushed the heart of God to remain silent and apart, but He did it because He loves us so fiercely that He couldn't stand the thought of being separated from us.

Don't forget: the crucifixion wasn't the end of the story. The resurrection was!

As Paul writes in Romans 8:

So, what do you think? With God on our side like this, how can we lose? If God didn't hesitate to put everything on the line for us, embracing our condition and exposing himself to the worst by sending his own Son, is there anything else he wouldn't gladly and freely do for us? And who would dare tangle with God by messing with one of God's chosen? Who would dare even to point a finger? The One who died for us—who was raised to life for us!—is in the presence of God at this very moment sticking up for us. Do you think anyone is going to be able to drive a wedge between us and Christ's love for us? There

is no way! Not trouble, not hard times, not hatred, not hunger,
not homelessness, not bullying threats, not backstabbing, not
even the worst sins listed in Scripture. . . . None of this fazes us
because Jesus loves us. I'm absolutely convinced that nothing—
nothing living or dead, angelic or demonic, today or tomorrow,
high or low, thinkable or unthinkable—absolutely *nothing* can
get between us and God's love because of the way that Jesus
our Master has embraced us. (vv. 31–39 MSG)

Bring Him your wounds. Show Him your scars. And trust Him,
who bore the scar of the cross for you, to make something beautiful out
of them.

May I pray for you?

Lord, please bless my friend who's reading right now. Give her the assur-
ance of Your presence and an awareness of Your forgiveness. In Your mercy,
take away the burden of guilt and shame she carries. Renew her mind so she
can focus on You. Give her the grace to begin again today . . . to believe that
You are always for her, not against her. May she one day stand amazed by
the way You have restored her life. Heal her wounded heart, Lord, so that
she can be a living testimony of Your awesome power. Amen.

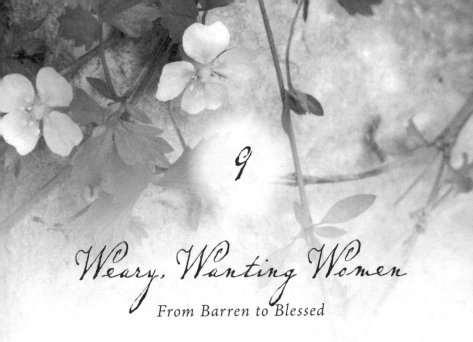

9

Weary, Wanting Women
From Barren to Blessed

❧ GENESIS 11, 24–25; 1 SAMUEL 1, 18; 2 SAMUEL ❧

TINA ❧ "When are you going to have a baby?" my family members asked (and, might I add, quite frequently). One year passed, two years passed, and then three. I wasn't sure my life was ready for that kind of responsibility. I was still working my way through college, and the thought of babies made the dream of a college diploma appear miles away.

Four years passed, five years, and six. Still no baby. Relatives began asking in a more intense and desperate manner. Their eyes gleamed with questions and the need for answers. "You've been married six years now," they said, as if we didn't know. The truth was, we hadn't even tried.

I can't help but reflect back on those years of *not* trying and compare them to the many couples who *were* trying—amazing couples, who for years sacrificed themselves, tolerated medications, endured countless doctor visits and everything else that went into desperately trying to conceive a child, only to see their hearts broken far too often. I can't imagine. I haven't personally experienced the ache or wound of such fruitless toil, but I have experienced it through friendships . . . and God's Word.

The Childless Ones

Sarah

Sarah is the first woman mentioned in the Bible as "childless." She married young Abram and together, with their family, "set out from Ur of the Chaldeans to go to Canaan. But when they came to Harran, they settled there" (Gen. 11:31). Imagine this beautiful young girl, newly married—and unable to conceive a child. It's easier to keep infertility a secret in today's world, but in her day, everyone knew. In biblical days, women lived in oversized fish bowls and spectators observed their pregnancy. Giving birth had meaning far beyond our experiences today. Having a child was important to their legacy, livelihood, and family duties.

Sarah's wound seeped into the crevices of her mind and produced bitterness and impatience. I use the word *mind* because that is where our bitterness often starts. What we think is going on, what we think should happen, how we perceive something, and our lack of understanding—all these add to the mixture of emotions we put in our hearts.

Dena and I shared more of Sarah's story in the chapter on Hagar, where we touched on the trouble Sarah faced because of her inability to produce an heir. Sarah's childless journey caused her to become bitter and impatient. Eventually, God did bless her with a child and they called him Isaac. Her conception came because God wanted to build a great nation.

Rebekah

After Sarah's death, Abraham sent his devoted servant to find a wife for Isaac. He wanted her to come from his own country and family, not from the Canaanites. After Abraham's clear directions, his servant prayed, "LORD, God of my master Abraham, make me successful today, and show kindness to my master Abraham" (Gen. 24:12).

And as the sun began to set, the women of the village came out to draw water from the well. "Before [the servant] had finished praying, Rebekah came out with her jar on her shoulder" (v. 15). She was not only beautiful to look at, but her heart held beauty as well. When the servant asked for water, she gave him a drink and drew water for his camels. That was the one sign the servant prayed for, in order to know which woman to bring back to Isaac.

Rebekah agreed to become Isaac's bride, but she had no idea of the hardships ahead. Along with the marriage came the pain of not being able to conceive a child. She too lived a childless life. Rebekah and her mother-in-law, Sarah, would have had much to talk about. It's sad they never had an opportunity to meet.

Rebekah continued her journey, displaying her inner beauty and kindness, though it would have been easy to become impatient like Sarah. Her strength came from something we all long for—a praying husband: "Isaac prayed to the LORD on behalf of his wife, because she was childless. The LORD answered his prayer, and his wife Rebekah became pregnant" . . . with twins! (Gen. 25:21). Her conception came after her husband's prayer, because of God's plan to build the nation of Israel.

Hannah

Hannah wed Elkanah, who had also married Peninnah. Imagine not only being the *other* woman, but the other woman who can't conceive! Hannah suffered the wound of being barren, as well as the wound of being mistreated because of her barrenness. Her emotional story is told in I Samuel. As I read through it, I can almost hear the pounding in her heart, her soul sodden with grief. "Because the LORD had closed Hannah's womb, her rival kept provoking her in order to irritate her.

This went on year after year. Whenever Hannah went up to the house of the LORD, her rival provoked her till she wept and would not eat" (1 Sam. 1:6–7).

Our souls mourn with Hannah and her suffering. But her tears and heart flowed in the right direction. "In her deep anguish Hannah prayed to the LORD, weeping bitterly. And she made a vow, saying, 'LORD Almighty, if you will only look on your servant's misery and remember me, and not forget your servant but give her a son, then I will give him to the LORD for all the days of his life'" (vv. 10–11). In her grief for a child, she turned to bargaining, a common stage in the grief process, pleading with God to do something.

> As she kept on praying to the LORD, Eli observed her mouth. Hannah was praying in her heart, and her lips were moving but her voice was not heard. Eli thought she was drunk and said to her, "How long are you going to stay drunk? Put away your wine."
>
> "Not so, my lord," Hannah replied, "I am a woman who is deeply troubled. . . . I have been praying here out of my great anguish and grief." (vv. 12–16)

Amazingly, the Lord answered Hannah's prayer. She too conceived and gave birth to a son she called Samuel. Her conception came after her great anguish and pleading, but the Scriptures are clear that she felt peace and acceptance even before she conceived a child. God used Samuel to build a great nation. Samuel anointed both Saul and David as kings over Israel.

An Empty Womb

Do you feel alone in your longing for a child? Do you wonder if the wound of an empty womb is yours and no one else's? Hannah, Rebekah, and Sarah must have felt that way. But there were others. Manoah's wife, Rachel, and Elizabeth also suffered many years with the inability to conceive, until one day, through God's blessing, all three gave birth to sons. Manoah's wife gave birth to Samson. Rachel birthed Joseph and died giving birth to Benjamin. Elizabeth birthed John the Baptist. Again we see God's great plan.

You might be asking, "That's great—but what happens to those women who are never able to have children? How do we cope? What do we do?" While some women are posing those questions, others might ask, "What happens when your circumstance doesn't allow it?" In today's world women adopt children without husbands. But what about those women longing for the tradition of having a spouse and together bringing a child into the world?

Several years back, my older sister developed uterine cancer. I sat beside her in the doctor's office and listened to the doctor explain the surgery, as well as the operation that would take away her ability to have children. As we exited the building, sorrow and loss draped over us like a big, black cape. Silence fell, and I gently turned in her direction to get a glimpse of how she was taking the news. Large tears formed in the corners of her eyes. I immediately placed my arms around her. "I'm so sorry and wish I could change this," I said.

She couldn't talk as tears trickled down her cheeks. "Are you worried about the surgery?" I asked. She shook her head no. In the silence I felt I needed to ask another question: "Did you want to have children?"

Her lip quivered and more tears followed. "Yes," she said.

Friend, we all have moments when we want to stomp our feet and shout, "Why?!" It's a wound so many women understand.

Sometimes, our circumstances don't allow us to have children. Michal was one such victim of circumstance.

King Saul had two daughters; Michal was the youngest. She fell in love with David and was given to him in marriage. Over time, Saul became fearful that David would usurp his throne and so he began a quest to kill David. Needless to say, the marriage between David and

Michal ended abruptly. Before Michal was able to conceive a child, David was out the door, running for his life.

Michal had helped him get away, and covered for his absence. She must have believed that David would one day send for her, but he did not.

He moved forward with his life and his two wives, who gave him many children, while Michal remained childless, pining for the man she loved. So many women today are yearning for a spouse and a child. It's difficult to understand why those desires haven't been met. Michal must have felt the same way.

After a while, Saul must have decided the marriage was null and void so he gave Michal to Paltiel, a suitable young man for his daughter. The two of them actually became quite happy with one another, but still Michal had not given birth to a child. She was very young, and I imagine her full of hope for the future. However, David finally defeated Saul, and his enemies asked to make peace. David agreed—but on one condition: Saul's men would give Michal back to David. After all, he had paid for her with one hundred Philistine foreskins, so in reality, David still owned her and possibly in his eyes, this was a way he could secure his way to the throne (since they had never divorced).

As if Michal's journey thus far wasn't painful enough, she was about to travel through another horrific wound. She was taken from her home, husband, and life. What a traumatic scene it was when her husband, Paltiel, dreadfully trailed behind her, weeping and groaning all the way to the city!

David didn't care for Michal, or the fact that she had loved him dearly. In the end, Michal basically became a prisoner in the house of David. She was stripped of her ability to have a child with her husband Paltiel, and though David could have given her children, he more than likely chose not to. The last recorded conversation between David and Michal left us with an understanding of the animosity between the two of them. "When [Michal] saw King David leaping and dancing before the LORD, she was filled with contempt for him" (2 Sam. 6:16 NLT).

Perhaps her bitterness came from David's unreturned love, snatching
her away from her new husband, or because David had not sent for her
sooner.

After David returned home, Michal chose to rebuke and confront
him ("in disgust," v. 20) for dancing nearly naked in front of other
women. David charged back, "'I was dancing before the LORD, who
chose me above your father and all his family! . . . Yes, and I am willing to look even more foolish than this, even to be humiliated in my
own eyes! But those servant girls you mentioned will indeed think I am
distinguished!'"

Yikes! What a moment. The passage goes on to say, "So Michal, the
daughter of Saul, remained childless throughout her entire life" (vv.
21–23 NLT). The Hebrew puts it this way, she "had no child." The word
"had" in Hebrew means *hayah*, which means "to come to pass, it happened, to be." We can assume that because of the issue between Michal
and David, "it came to be" that she remained lonely and childless until
the day she died.

Whatever the circumstance, not having the opportunity to bear children can feel just as painful as being barren. When our desires continue
to go unfilled, it's a powerful wound. Many of you right now are pon-
dering your painful circumstances. What do we do with such wounds?

An Untimely Circumstance

I recently spoke with a friend and listened to her share about having
ovarian cancer. She went into surgery understanding that the doctors
were going to remove everything she would need to conceive a child.
At the age of twenty-one, ten months before her wedding day, Kara
faced the pain of becoming barren. That's enough to cause anyone to
become angry with God. But during the surgery, something miraculous happened. The doctors realized they could possibly save one of her
ovaries. They made their way to the waiting room and consulted with
her future husband. His emotions carried him to a place he really didn't

want to go. After prayer and conversation with the family, they chose to go ahead and try to save the ovary.

The surgery was a success. Doctors removed all of the cancer and were able to save one of the ovaries; however, the hope of having a child was still extremely dim. It would take a miracle. Kara had much to sort through, and as she did, she concluded that there was one thing she still held on to. Above all else, she loved God and trusted Him. If He chose to allow her to have a child, she would feel privileged and blessed beyond measure. However, if for some reason she was not able to conceive, she would be heartbroken, but continue to trust that God had her best interest at heart. She would continue to love Him.

Kara is an amazing woman, like so many others who face the same issue. Some women may feel guilty and ashamed for becoming angry at God. He understands your heart, though He doesn't want you to stay sunken in bitterness.

Birthing the Glory
Isaiah talks about the future glory of Zion:

"Sing, barren woman, you who never bore a child; burst into song, shout for joy, you who were never in labor; because more are the children of the desolate woman than of her who has a husband," says the LORD. "Enlarge the place of your tent, stretch your tent curtains wide, do not hold back; lengthen your cords, strengthen your stakes." (Isa. 54:1–2)

The barren woman Isaiah refers to is the city of Jerusalem. She had a reputation for living in sin. Cities and nations in the Old Testament were often referred to as barren, especially when they produced no righteous fruit. The hand of blessing had been removed from Jerusalem, and the city was in complete despair. But God wanted to change that. He wanted to show mercy and give her a covenant of peace and fruitfulness.

God wanted to saturate the sinful city with His sacred presence and bring the people into a place where He dwells.

God urged the barren woman to sing because the fruit that she would soon produce would be far greater than that of the one who had a husband. God was about to bring the barren woman into His presence!

I love this metaphor because it touches close to home. God does the same for me, and for you. And please hear me, I am not calling you a sinful Jerusalem, or saying sin is the reason for your circumstances. Far from it. I'm saying that God promises to change your barren heart, just as He did Jerusalem's. Because of His life-changing grace, you *will* produce amazing offspring.

Yes, the wound of not being able to conceive hurts. It feels so wrong. But let me encourage you: your pain is not without reason. God promises that if you remain close to Him (the Vine), you will bear fruit in other ways. Perhaps you will adopt a baby who is desperate for wonderful parents. And what a privilege if God sets you aside to care for that little person!

Maybe you will start a children's ministry or work in the one at your church. Maybe God will call you to work at a day care center where parents have to leave their children for hours at a time—or you will one day travel overseas to minister in an orphanage. God may even use your brokenness to produce spiritual offspring through a ministry whose fruit "no eye has seen . . . no ear has heard, and . . . no human mind has conceived" (1 Cor. 2:9).

My dear friends, my heart aches with you. But please know, God has a divine purpose for your life.

In six different lines, Psalm 113 encourages us to praise the Lord! But how can we praise Him when our hearts are so filled with longing for a child? Trying to find peace and comfort on our own may be impossible, but through Christ, all things are possible. The psalmist continues, "The LORD is exalted over all the nations, his glory above the heavens. Who is like the LORD our God, the One who sits enthroned on high, who stoops down to look on the heavens and the earth?" Yes, God truly sees! "He raises the poor from the dust and lifts the needy from the ash heap; he seats them with princes, with the princes of his people. He settles the childless woman in her home as a happy mother of children. Praise the Lord" (vv. 4–9).

You see, God will settle the childless woman in her home *as* a happy mother with children. He doesn't promise children. He promises to settle our hearts and give us joy *as* that of a woman with children.

That is the glory He promises, sisters. So get ready! As Isaiah says, "Do not hold back" (54:2). Enlarge your ministry, stretch yourself, lengthen your abilities, and strengthen your gifting.

Your New Jerusalem is coming!

DENA ✖ I held the phone receiver tightly as the nurse on the other end of the line said, "Congratulations! You're pregnant."

When I didn't respond, she asked, "Is this not good news?"

Taking a deep breath, I answered, "Well, I've been bleeding for about three weeks, and the doctor said that if I was pregnant, I was also probably already miscarrying."

"I'm so sorry," she said softly.

And so began one of the hardest experiences I'd ever gone through. As it turned out, I *was* miscarrying, and I soon became a frequent guest in my ob-gyn's office for weekly blood work, sitting in the waiting room with several *very* pregnant women. Talk about pouring salt on a wound! It seemed that my body didn't want to get rid of the baby quickly, so I was forced to visit the office for what seemed like months. (I'm sure it was just a few times.)

The year was 1996, and my hubby and I were newlyweds and seminary students. Since my childhood—one spent teaching my stuffed animals, putting my dolls down for naps, and bossing around my younger brother—I'd longed to be a mom. Miscarriage wasn't something I ever pictured going through.

The phone call, and subsequent doctor visits, sent me reeling. I was convinced I had done something wrong, and I felt terribly guilty. My hubby, Carey, also felt the loss deeply—and shared my frustration at the hurtful comments we received.

The weekend after I lost our baby, Carey and I drove to an amphitheater an hour from our apartment. We served as cast members in a life of Christ production, and Carey played a lead role. After the cast-wide prayer meeting that preceded the show—in which I tearfully asked for prayer—I received permission to sit out of the performance and watch. As the overture began, I took my seat in the audience.

During the first scene, a grandfather and his two grandchildren explore the Texas hill country and make a campfire. The grandfather tells his grandkids about the life of Jesus as singers, actors, and dancers reenact the story around them.

With a heavy heart, feeling very much alone, I watched as the grandchildren noticed an abandoned cemetery. "This one was just a baby," said one of the children as she pointed to a tombstone.

"I think it's sad when babies die," said the other child. I sat up straighter. I had never paid attention to those lines before.

Tears began to fall as I sensed God showing me, in a very specific way, that He saw my pain. He knew what I was going through—and unlike my well-meaning friends and family members, He knew exactly what to say.

"It is sad," agreed the grandfather character. "But every baby is special to God . . . and one baby was so special, He was promised by prophets." The production continued as actors portraying prophets began to sing on stage . . . but I wasn't paying attention anymore.

Instead, I was thanking God and shaking my head in amazement at the comfort I'd just received from a very thoughtful heavenly Father.

My baby was special to Him—and I was too.

Good Grief

Before her health became poor, when Tracey Cotson heard the word *grief*, her immediate thoughts were of someone having lost a person close to them. It was not a word she wanted to get acquainted with personally. And grief being good? *No way*, she thought.

"I always assumed that grieving was something that happened only after a person in your life died," Tracey said. "I didn't see it as a process that one goes through in order to move forward. I also used to assume that grief was linear, but no longer."

In February 2001, she started going to the doctor for unexplained symptoms and was finally diagnosed with an autoimmune disorder more than a year later. At their wedding, Tracey and her new husband thought the worst was over.

However, after their first child, Miles, was born in April 2006, Tracey had complications and wasn't able to leave the hospital until July 19. In September, when Miles was five months old, she began to realize all that she had missed in his young life up to that point: "I remember breaking down in the shower one evening, sobbing uncontrollably because I hadn't been able to celebrate my first Mother's Day, hadn't carried him home for the first time, hadn't been able to breastfeed like I'd wanted, hadn't even taken one picture of him until he was four months old. I had dreamed of taking photos of him as a tiny newborn. I had missed that."

The couple started trying to have another baby in March 2008 and still haven't been able to conceive. Tracey has discovered that grief is not linear: "There can be ten steps forward and one hundred steps back. There can be two steps up and four steps down. There can be a valley after a valley—it's not always valley-mountain-valley-mountain. Your pain is your pain, and it can be a lonely place if you let it—and sometimes even if you don't."

Tracey explained that she's handled her grief over secondary infertility and her illness in both positive and negative ways. One thing she has learned, "sometimes grudgingly," is that she will never be the exact same person she used to be. Life looks different to Tracey now, but she also believes that parts of her are better because she went through trials. She's also noticed that her joys are sweeter because of her sorrows. "My pain is deep, but I hold the tiniest moments close to my heart. I don't think I would have done that, had things been easier," she explained.

"Grief is not a friend of mine, but lately I'm seeing that I have to sit with it in order to heal. There is no other way. I could try to avoid it my entire life, but what kind of life would that be? I am tired of pain, and I know I will grieve certain things until I die, but the deep sadness is something I must sit with so that I can move on. And though I am not at the end of it, I have at least moved in a positive direction."

That, Tracey noted, is *good grief.*

From Depressed to Obsessed

"The chances of you getting pregnant are slim," a doctor told Charity Ourso one afternoon. The words stung her to the core. She and her husband had been trying to get pregnant with their second child for two years. All the tests the doctors ran had come back showing that nothing was wrong, and physicians had no explanation for the couple's inability to conceive.

Charity said, "It had always been a desire of mine, since I was a little girl, to be a mom to two children. Being raised in a home with two parents and a younger brother, we made up the fantastic four. I knew at a young age that my calling in life was to be a wife and a mother, and having a family of four, to me, was the perfect picture."

"I don't understand!" Charity told the Lord. "Why me?" She was hungry to find out some answers and to understand the will of God, so she turned to God's Word.

However, the more she clung to God's Word, the harder Satan fought her. Soon, Charity was becoming depressed over her situation and noticed the joys of everyday life slipping away.

"I felt as if the Lord had let me down. I loved Him, worshipped Him, faithfully served Him, and cried out to Him many times in prayer. How could He say no to this one desire? I felt alone, isolated, and shut out on the blessings of God. Satan used this lonely time to cause self-doubt in my roles as a wife and mother and doubt in my heavenly Father."

Has Satan accused you like he did Charity? Has his malevolent voice hissed, "God is unhappy with you . . . You're a loser, a fraud . . . God is punishing you . . . Could you really serve a God who's let you down?"

Perhaps he has sidled up to you and suggested that instead of wanting the best for you, God has been keeping His best from you—just like he did with Eve in the garden: "The serpent told the Woman, 'You won't die. God knows that the moment you eat from that tree, you'll see what's really going on. You'll be just like God, knowing everything, ranging all the way from good to evil'" (Gen. 3:4–5 MSG).

If he's been whispering this same lie to you, you know how desperate you can feel when those thoughts start swirling in your head.

Before long, Charity's depression turned into obsession with pregnancy. She said, "I started writing down every time someone I knew would announce they were pregnant. (I stopped when it reached twenty-two.) I would notice women who walked down the street, at the mall or in restaurants, and count how many children they had. I would notice women who were pregnant. I wanted to feel the excitement of each stage of pregnancy again. I wanted to share in the joys of baby talk and bulging bellies. I longed to feel all those special moments of carrying a baby again. Yet, each month that went by God said no."

Thankfully, God used Charity's husband, John, to encourage her and convict her. "He told me to remember my first love, Jesus, and asked me if I were making pregnancy an idol. His words opened my eyes to the sin I was living in. I needed to rest in the assurance that God had a plan."

Dear friend, God has a plan for you too! He wants to give you peace, grace, and the assurance that He will never, ever leave you.

Charity's prayers for a second child have yet to be answered. But as her mind cleared, and she turned to God's Word for comfort and peace, He started to heal her heart.

He can do the same for you. Even if you feel that He's not listening, He is. Our heavenly Father longs for you to turn to Him, not away from Him, in the midst of your grief. He wants to take you in His arms and sing sweet songs of love to you.

You may feel scared to come to God because you're angry at Him. Just remember, healthy relationships thrive on honesty, and our relationship to God is no different. When we come to Him as we are—without pretense, walls, or preconceived notions of what He will or won't do—He moves us from where we are spiritually to where we need to be.

Andi Shaw shared with God that she felt "cursed" when she couldn't conceive a child. "I saw in Scripture that a woman who had the ability to bear children was 'blessed,' so one who was unable to do so must be the opposite. I alternately cried out to and railed at God over this, wondering what made me worse than other women. I alternated between hope for my personal healing and extreme discouragement when it didn't happen."

Her grieving process took some time. Like many women who've struggled with infertility, Andi's hopes rose when people prayed for her or assertively pronounced, "You can have children; don't give up!" Thus, the death of hope was a slow and gradual one.

She says, "I had to constantly remind myself that I live in a fallen world where disease and physical imperfections exist, but that—through Christ Jesus—I still am accepted, beloved, treasured, and made holy and precious to Abba God. As a Christ-follower and child of God, I *am* blessed, and even though I may not see God's plan, I choose to trust that He has good things planned for me. My future will not include biological children, but it does *not* mean I am less of a woman. I am still precious to God."

Andi also realized that she could broaden her definition of motherhood. She has been a school teacher, a military chaplain, and a youth worker. "In all these ways I have mothered, nurtured, and cared for others. I was unable to hear this from other people, even those with the best intentions; it was only something I could receive from God, and it took time to accept that I am as much a mother as any woman with biological children."

And now, Andi meets with other women who are walking through infertility. She notes, "I must be careful what I say to them. It's best to let the other woman lead the conversation, not offering platitudes, but simply listening to her and answering direct questions as I am able."

She also offers caution to those who want to comfort someone in the midst of the struggle to conceive biological children. "If you haven't personally experienced infertility, guard what you say to someone walking through it, especially if you're personally uncomfortable with the topic or situation. Some of the most callous words spoken to me have come from people who were uncomfortable with my situation and offered platitudes as a means to escape the topic."

Andi advises simplicity and brevity over length. "You might say, I can't understand what you're walking through and can't even imagine how difficult it is. I *can* say you are a blessing to [me, this church, our women's group, etc.], and [I, we] love you very much!" *What great advice!* As someone who's been wounded by those who tried to comfort me, I can see without a doubt that simple presence is often the best present.

Beloved sister, God's presence is always available to us, whatever we are struggling with. Are you aching, like the women in our chapter, to bear a child? Does your unfulfilled desire seem like a cruel joke God is playing on you? I wish I could give you a hug right now, and tell you how much He loves you; how delighted He is in you; and how completely He longs to transform your grief into glory.

One day, you will no longer be barren. In heaven, you and I will be surrounded not only by our family but by the spiritual children we've shepherded into the kingdom.

In this lifetime, if we hand over our hearts to Him, He will begin a transformative work in us that others will point to and say, "Look at the work God has done!" Just as God made a great nation out of the once-barren wombs of Sarah and Rebekah, just as He gave Hannah the child she longed for, and gifted Elizabeth with a remarkable son who became the one to prepare the way for Jesus, so will He create out of us, His dear daughters, a people who will display His glory.

Pay close attention now:

> I'm creating new heavens and a new earth.
> All the earlier troubles, chaos, and pain
> are things of the past, to be forgotten.
> Look ahead with joy.
> Anticipate what I'm creating:
> I'll create Jerusalem as sheer joy,
> create my people as pure delight. . . .
> No more sounds of weeping in the city,
> no cries of anguish;
> No more babies dying in the cradle,
> or old people who don't enjoy a full lifetime;
> One-hundredth birthdays will be considered normal—
> anything less will seem like a cheat. (Isa. 65:17–20 MSG)

Now that is a promise to hold on to!

10

Ichabod's Mother

From Burdened to Bitter

❧ 1 Samuel 4 ❧

TINA ❧ As a pastor's wife, I sometimes find myself staring into the windows of other women's lives. "How much more can they take, Lord?" I ask as I pray for them. Have you said those words lately? There are those who seem to suffer more than others; whose tragedies seem to collide one with another. Their lives appear battered, beaten, and bewildered. Their troubles seem unjust and unwarranted. Ocean waves shove them here and there; they are thrashed against hard stone walls. It's painful to watch.

During my senior year in high school, while working part-time as a dispatcher for the sheriff's department, I received a call that a house was on fire. As I began to connect the frantic woman to the fire department, I realized the voice seemed familiar. It was my older sister. The house burning was my own! We lost almost everything that year. The water damaged what the fire didn't take. It was difficult to swallow, knowing we had very little from the start. Our poverty level ranked near the bottom, and we were definitely one of those families who knew what it felt like to fight to survive—and humble ourselves for help.

After the fire, we learned the insurance company my father paid into ran off with our money—leaving us without home insurance. I am not sure how we were able to rebuild, but somehow we did. Three months later, a large storm rose up, and baseball-sized hail pummeled our house. The intense pounding sounded like sledgehammers breaking through walls. The windows broke, sending shards of glass flying. My brothers caught the television, keeping it from tumbling over, as my mother grabbed anything else that might break. *Is this a tornado?* I wondered. The lights went out and we cowered in the corners. The next morning, we stepped outside and stared at the recently applied siding, which still held its new smell. It looked like someone had taken a machine gun and shot it to pieces. Our hearts sank. We still didn't carry insurance. *Why is this happening, God?* we asked.

Sometimes it feels as if the weight of the world has fallen upon us. The heaviness suffocates and blinds us. We cannot see the view from where we are looking—but God can.

Do You Know My Name?

Does it ever feel like God has forgotten your name, that you don't exist at all? I wonder if Ichabod's mother felt the same way. She is someone Ichabod never had the opportunity to meet because he was born in the center of a tragedy.

She is mentioned just briefly in the Old Testament, and the writer never mentioned her name. How sad! I wish I knew what to call her. What kind of journey did she walk? It seemed difficult and tiresome.

For the sake of the story, let's give her a name—"Amasa," which in Hebrew means "burden." The name seems fitting, for she lived a life of hardship.

We don't know much about her. I wonder where she came from, the color of her eyes, and the beauty of her skin. I have no idea what made her laugh, cry, or cause her heart to beat with excitement. Did she carry on the everyday duties of an Israelite wife or enjoy a special craft? What passions did she embrace? Was she able to live life in abundance, or did she live it dreadfully, in despair?

What we do know is she married into a family that held a position of great honor and respect. Amasa married Phinehas, a Levite who lived in the city of Shiloh and served as a priest in the tabernacle. In essence, she became what I would call a pastor's wife. She was the daughter-in-law of Eli, the great high priest.

What a blessing to be the daughter-in-law of a high priest! Although my father-in-law was not a high priest, he served as a missionary and pastor for many years. I can imagine what it may have felt like for Amasa to marry into that kind of family. There is a sense of admiration and high regard that comes with that title. She married into a name of importance, but something happened along the way that changed everything.

Eli had an amazing opportunity to do great things for the Lord, including raise his children and have them serve alongside him. Many fathers would value the opportunity, but somewhere along the line, Eli failed at the chance to become a great father. He failed at the opportunity to instruct, discipline, and educate his children about the God who placed them in such a unique and wonderful position of service. Because of that, many people were wounded—particularly Amasa.

Wounds Exposed

The Lord felt Eli honored his sons more than he honored Him. The Lord asked, "Why do you honor your sons more than me by fattening yourselves on the choice parts of every offering made by my people Israel?" (1 Sam. 2:29).

The Bible tells us that Eli's sons, Hophni and Phinehas, "were scoundrels; they had no regard for the LORD. Now it was the practice of the priests that, whenever any of the people offered a sacrifice, the priest's servant would come with a three-pronged fork in his hand while the meat was being boiled and would plunge the fork into the pan or kettle or caldron or pot. Whatever the fork brought up the priest would take for himself" (vv. 12–14). But as the Israelite people began offering their sacrifices, Hophni and Phinehas asked for it before it was cooked. If anyone refused to hand it over, they took it by force. The God who sees declared that the two men treated the offering with "contempt" and He took their sinning very seriously (v. 17).

Think about Amasa's wound as rumors swirled throughout the city. Imagine the embarrassment and humiliation she carried as the wife of one of the priests who dishonored the Lord and His people. Not only did rumors circle about the offerings, but the two brothers had an issue with sexual integrity as well. The brothers, who worked at the tabernacle, slept with the women who also worked at the entrance of the tent of meeting.

"Now Eli, who was very old, heard about everything his sons were doing to all Israel and how they slept with the women who served at the entrance to the tent of meeting. So he said to them, 'Why do you do such things? I hear from all the people about these wicked deeds of yours. No, my sons; the report I hear spreading among the LORD's people is not good'" (vv. 22–24). If others in the town heard the rumors about Hophni and Phinehas, Amasa did as well. How many women can relate to having husbands who brazenly sleep with other women, who openly break the law and abuse their position? Amasa despaired.

I often question how my mother felt about my father, who had qualities similar to Eli's sons. Hophni and Phinehas lived a life of sin, broke the law, and had no regard for God; my father did the same. In his younger years, my dad joined his brother in a quest to make more money through armed robbery and burglary. My dad drove the getaway car for two men who committed the robberies. The three of them had a system where they could get in and out of houses with precision and accuracy, carrying valuables of all kinds. My father stashed the stolen goods and sold them when the time was right. Newspapers wrote about the trio and police officers chased them. Their crimes didn't last a week or a month, but years. My mother, who had been raised in a Christian home, looked the other way to keep her family together. I'm sure she didn't know what to do—much like Amasa.

Before long, the men were wanted throughout Texas. The Texas Rangers chased my father all over the state. That's one reason we moved so much. My dad, the fugitive, took his entire family with him. Perhaps it wasn't as dramatic for Amasa, but I have no doubt my mother can relate to the humility and fear this biblical woman experienced. When a sinful lifestyle is exposed—especially when the sin is ongoing—others see, know, and are affected by it.

All Things Come to an End

Day after day, Amasa lived with the wound of her husband's sins and the devastation it brought to her and her family. Because of Phinehas and Hophni's unwillingness to turn from their sinful lifestyle, God decided to put an end to it.

At some point, war broke out between the Israelites and the Philistines: "The Philistines deployed their forces to meet Israel, and as the battle spread, Israel was defeated by the Philistines, who killed about four thousand of them on the battlefield" (1 Sam. 4:2). The Israelites could not understand why God didn't help them. Someone suggested they bring the ark of the covenant to the battlefield. They believed God would protect them through that act and turn the battle in their favor. Soon the ark of the covenant arrived, along with Hophni and Phinehas. "So the Philistines fought, and the Israelites were defeated. . . . The slaughter was very great; Israel lost thirty thousand foot soldiers. The ark of God was captured, and Eli's two sons, Hophni and Phinehas, died" (vv. 10–11).

Eli's large frame hung over the sides of the chair as he turned his face toward the city gate. A thick cloud covered his eyes and left him with dark shadows. *Is anyone coming?* He listened for footsteps approaching his way. *Finally*, he thought as someone drew near. But the good news

Eli hoped to receive from the front didn't arrive. And when he heard the report about his sons and the ark of God, Eli fell backward off his chair, broke his neck, and died.

Amasa was about to learn that her husband, brother-in-law, and father-in-law died on the same day—within hours of one another. As if she needed more distress, she would also learn that the ark of the covenant had been captured by their enemies. The sacred box that carried the Ten Commandments and kept the Spirit of the Lord near was now gone. She must have been frightened when she realized that the ark had been under the protection of her husband when it was captured.

In the midst of her anguish, Amasa carried a gift—a baby. Her physical fatigue matched her emotional misery, because it was near the time for her to deliver. The news of what happened to her father-in-law, husband, brother-in-law, and the ark of the covenant was too much to bear. The Bible says, "She went into labor and gave birth, but was overcome by her labor pains." As she lay dying, "the women attending her said, 'Don't despair; you have given birth to a son.' But she did not respond or pay any attention. She named the boy Ichabod, saying, 'The Glory has departed from Israel'" (vv. 19–21).

Has the Glory Departed?

We've all faced seasons of tragedies where it feels as if the glory of the Lord has departed from us. The deaths of Eli and his family members were shattering and tragic. Ichabod's mother's life ended in defeat—but ours doesn't have to. In her last moments, she suffered greatly . . . not only emotionally and physically, but also spiritually. The midwives had it right when they said, "Don't despair; you have given birth to a son." That son would carry on the family name, legacy, and birthright. Her family lineage would live. In a sense, she would live!

In those few seconds after her baby's birth and before her death, Ichabod's mother could have shouted *kabowd*, which in Hebrew means "Glory!" She could have shouted out a name that meant *God is coming,*

You are blessed, or *Lord be praised!* Instead, in her woundedness, she called the boy *Iy-kabowd* or *Ichabod,* which means "no glory."

How often, in our wounded moments, do we outwardly confess our bitterness and pass it on to our children, family, friends, and coworkers? How often, in the middle of our hurts, do we rise up and speak against God, rather than for Him? As my husband and I searched the Scriptures we found that *kabowd* is mentioned two hundred times and *Iy-kabowd* (Ichabod) is referenced two times. Ichabod's mother got it wrong.

Though our situations may feel unfavorable and unfortunate, is it possible to trust God enough to believe He is working in all things, on our behalf? Job, though he lost everything, still rose up, "tore his robe and shaved his head. Then he fell to the ground in worship and said: 'Naked I came from my mother's womb, and naked I will depart. The LORD gave and the LORD has taken away; may the name of the LORD be praised.' In all this, Job did not sin by charging God with wrongdoing" (Job 1:20–22). Job did not sin—he worshipped.

Asaph, another worshipper of God, wrote in Psalm 77 how we all have felt:

> I cried out to God for help;
>   I cried out to God to hear me.
> When I was in distress, I sought the Lord;
>   at night I stretched out untiring hands,
>   and I would not be comforted . . . .
> Will the Lord reject forever?
>   Will he never show his favor again?
> Has his unfailing love vanished forever?
>   Has his promise failed for all time?
> Has God forgotten to be merciful?
>   Has he in anger withheld his compassion? (vv. 1–2, 7–9)

Asaph questioned, as we do, but his song did not end there. He did something we all should do in the midst of our trials and tribulation— he focused on the goodness of God. He determined, by an act of his will (and not his emotions), to recount the true character of the Most High. He chose to "remember the deeds of the LORD," the "miracles of long ago" (v. 11). He thought about every little thing God did in his life and *meditated* on it. Asaph had to go back and remind himself of the good things about God.

When we are living in a dark situation, and when life seems to pile up on us, how do we make sense of anything? We must step back and remind ourselves of those times when we did see God working—in our lives or others' lives. After Asaph questioned and reflected back, he then declared, "Your ways, God, *are* holy. What god is as great as our God?" (v. 13, italics added). That mind-set is what kept Asaph from staying and living in great despair. That mind-set is what caused Asaph to praise God rather than curse Him.

My friends, life doesn't seem fair, and at times it's not. Far too often our burdens turn us bitter. However, if we can somehow remind ourselves that in truth, God is good, God does care, and God does love, then perhaps we will be able to move forward in hope. We will also pass that hope on to the generations who come behind us. Instead of leaving our children with the bitterness of Ichabod—we can leave them with the glory of God.

DENA ❧ The last half decade has been full of change for our little family of four. A dear friend tragically lost his life in a motorcycle accident. His sudden death plunged a company (into which we had invested our lives and money) into turmoil, which cost us both money and relationships. We grieved—and experienced hurt, confusion, and frustration.

Our stressors also included several job changes for both my husband and me, and a total of four moves in five years. We've bought and sold three houses (well, we *bought* three houses . . . one is yet to sell, so we're renting it). Finally, both my dad and my father-in-law underwent major heart surgery within a few months. And if all this wasn't enough, I was going through perimenopause while my oldest son turned into a teenager (aka Dr. Jekyll and Mr. Hyde).

Can you say emotional rollercoaster?

On certain days, I asked God if the craziness of our current situation would ever ease up. *Lord*, I said, *I like double loops and corkscrews as much as anyone, but we've been through the ups and downs now a few times—and the thrill is gone. Nausea has set in.*

I didn't want to be like Ichabod's mother—turning my back on God because I felt like I didn't deserve my circumstances. I longed to be obedient, even in the difficulties. And so I prayed continually for strength, and I kept seeking Him . . . even when He seemed very, very quiet on the subject of when (or if) we might be done with the "desert" we were in.

And every time I cried out to Him, He answered. Sometimes He reminded me of a Scripture passage that ministered profoundly to me. Songs came on the radio that seemed to have been written just for my situation. Friends and family members called, texted, and emailed at perfect moments, when I couldn't seem to take another step or cry another tear. He was faithful. So, so faithful.

Six months ago, God led my husband back into full-time ministry— and moved us back to a place we love, among people we treasure, who treasure us. It feels as if we are coming out of the desert and into an oasis. We are grateful beyond words. And we can see, in hindsight, that He's been preparing us all along to minister more effectively to those who have experienced tumult and tragedy.

People like Nichole, who experienced intense suffering for well over a decade.

A Soul-Testing Illness

When she was just four years old, Nichole developed the autoimmune disorder known as Crohn's disease. For Nichole, the disease has been painful, progressive, and often times debilitating.

Although her family had not been religious until Nichole's diagnosis, her mother decided to raise her children with faith as an anchor, so the family began attending church. Before long, their entire family was involved in church and was having family devotionals and personal quiet times consistently. Nichole is thankful that her illness caused her family to turn toward God—not curse Him.

She says, "As my disease progressed, I clung to my faith. When I felt all alone, like none of my peers could understand the agony that I was experiencing, God became my one constant, the one that I could cry out to in the middle of the night when the pain kept me awake, the only one who could relate to my embarrassment when I was sick in front of my peers."

Despite being treated by some of the best specialists in the world, and taking all of the latest medications, Nichole's disease progressed to the point that by the time she was a sophomore in high school, scar tissue had almost completely blocked her large intestine. Specialists recommended that her colon be removed. After coming out of surgery, she expected to feel better. Unfortunately, she had complications and had to undergo two more surgeries.

Nichole was devastated, until she stumbled upon a verse in Job. In the passage preceding Job 23:10, Job feels discouraged—looking for God, but not finding Him. Finally, Job exclaims, "But he knows the way that I take; when he has tested me, I will come forth as gold." Nichole clung to that verse.

"My disease stubbornly refused to stay in remission and recurred throughout the course of the next thirteen years, through four more surgeries, a leukemia drug, and IV infusions. Job 23:10 carried me through many hard times when I felt alone. There were so many times that I couldn't see Him in the midst of my circumstances."

Nichole has now been disease-free for eight years, but she believes, "When I was ill, He was developing my character and had plans for me for things that are still to come."

Just as He did for Nichole, God can use our pain to transform us—if we will allow Him to.

What about you? Have you lost hope? Are your thoughts filled with doubt and pain? Maybe you're tempted to despair, fearing that God has left you, never to return.

Dear one, you are not alone. And God has not gone anywhere, even if it feels that way. I urge you to believe that—even if you have to pray, "God, give me the faith to have faith."

When God Seems Absent

A woman told me that one year ago, one of her two best friends committed suicide. She said, "She was married with three young children. And it really threw me. To be honest, I found myself doubting my faith and God's goodness. I had prayed for her for countless hours. She was a believer, and it seemed that God had abandoned her. I knew that wasn't really true, but I couldn't understand it. I still can't fathom the purpose in all of it, but God has brought me out of a terribly dark place."

She continued, "I want to remind women going through a tragedy that causes them to doubt, that God will bring them through. And that though they may never have all the answers to *why*, God in His grace will, over time, heal them and renew their faith."

Why them? Satan whispers into my ears when others face impossible circumstances. *Why me?* he tempts me to ask when I hurt, especially when my wound seems too big to ever heal. At a ladies' retreat for which I led music, the speaker—pastor's wife Amy McGown—led a session about the "gift" of pain. She said, "At first, it looks like a curse. But if we trust God, instead of our feelings, He will give us peace—and more."

Amy, a licensed Christian counselor, reminded us about the woman with long-term bleeding, a story that has always moved me, recorded in Mark 5:25–34 and Luke 8:42–48. Because of the woman's medical condition, everyone shunned her. She had spent all her time, money, and energy trying to find a cure for her disease. She was isolated, embarrassed, frustrated, depressed, and broke.

The woman rushed through a crowd where Jesus was walking. Scripture says that she touched the hem of His garment, most likely pushing through the throng of people to get to Jesus. In that moment, Jesus felt the power go out of Him—and she was immediately healed.

Show Up—Don't Give Up

Using the story of this desperate woman as an example, Amy urged us to press into Jesus, instead of running from pain. "Show up, don't give up!" she said. "Don't quit going to church or stop studying the Bible just because God hasn't answered you in the ways you think He should. And latch on to Jesus, instead of lashing out in frustration. Jeremiah 29:13 says that those who seek God *will* find Him."

Finally, Amy encouraged wounded women to keep their eyes on (what should be) the ultimate goal of our journey—knowing Jesus intimately. "Pain doesn't sideline us unless we let it," she said.

Do you consider pain a curse? Or with God's help, will you determine to unwrap this unlikely gift . . . and in the process, become closer to His heart?

As the apostle Paul wrote:

> Yes, all the things I once thought were so important are gone from my life. Compared to the high privilege of knowing Christ Jesus as my Master, firsthand, everything I once thought I had going for me is insignificant. . . . I've dumped it all in the trash so that I could embrace Christ and be embraced by him. I didn't want some petty, inferior brand of righteousness that comes from keeping a list of rules when I could get the robust kind that comes from trusting Christ—*God's* righteousness. I

gave up all that inferior stuff so I could know Christ personally, experience his resurrection power, be a partner in his suffering, and go all the way with him to death itself. If there was
any way to get in on the resurrection from the dead, I wanted
to do it. I'm not saying that I have this all together, that I have
it made. But I am well on my way, reaching out for Christ, who
has so wondrously reached out for me. Friends, don't get me
wrong: By no means do I count myself an expert in all of this,
but I've got my eye on the goal, where God is beckoning us
onward—to Jesus. I'm off and running, and I'm not turning
back. (Phil. 3:8–14 MSG)

Surviving—with God's Help

My sweet friend, Shaela Manross, was only seventeen years old
when she unwillingly joined that fellowship of suffering. Because of the
actions of a madman, her life changed in one terrifying second. She says,
"Growing up in church, there are certain Bible verses that are quoted
whenever something tragic happens: Romans 8:28 ('In all things God
works for the good of those who love him') and Romans 8:37 ('We are
more than conquerors') are two of them. I had heard those verses time
and time again. Of course, I knew the words were true. I knew that God
had a plan for my life, and I trusted that He would lead me on that path
He had marked out for me. But knowing that and experiencing it are
two very different things."

Shaela was a new member of the small youth group at Wedgwood
Baptist Church in Fort Worth, Texas, on September 15, 1999. On that
fateful evening, she drove to her church to meet up with the group.

She says, "A few songs into the worship service, I thought someone
was popping balloons in the back of the sanctuary. When I turned
around, I didn't see colorful balloons; instead, I saw fire shooting out
the barrel of a small handheld gun."

Instinct took over, and Shaela flew to the floor. She grabbed the freshman boy next to her and told him to get down. He looked at her, confused, and asked, "This is the skit in the program, isn't it?"

About that time, the boy on the other side of Shaela dropped his video camera and fell to the ground. She says, "I looked at him in horror. Then a loud bang, followed by tiny pieces of metal hitting my legs, brought me up from under the pew. Was it a bomb? I wasn't sure."

She looked again toward the boy with the video camera. He was dead.

"I began to sob. I turned back to the boy to my left, telling him: 'Stay down. This isn't a skit.'"

In a matter of minutes—it seemed like much longer—students began slowly rising from their pews as they realized that the shooter had shot himself. Shaela says, "An adult yelled at us to get away from the church, so we all began rushing out. I stopped as I passed the boy with the camera, wondering if I should try to carry him or leave him there. I left—a decision that's plagued me for years."

The events outside were a blur: sirens, lights, helicopters overhead. "It was a hive of activity. A newspaper reporter took a picture and asked me for my name and age. Much later, I found my parents and they took me to the police station. The night seemed to never end, but finally, I was released to go home," she says.

In the months after the shooting, Shaela received many cards, flowers, words of encouragement, and condolences. However, she felt nothing but pain. She was constantly afraid. Noises, shadows—they all brought back memories from that tragic night. "I couldn't sleep because of nightmares, and I was terrified of the dark. I was seventeen years old and my mom had to sleep with me, holding my hand, with a lamp on all night. After missing school because I couldn't handle hearing lockers slam shut or reading biology books about the human anatomy, my parents put me in counseling."

Through the words of truth from her Christian counselor, God began to remind Shaela that He still had a plan. "His plan didn't change when His only Son was nailed to the cross (a reminder from Pastor Al Meredith of Wedgwood Baptist Church the week after the shooting), and it wouldn't change now because of that dreadful night. And what God assured me of was that His plan *for me* is perfect. He holds the universe in His hand, and yet He has a plan for my life and He will indeed lead me through."

Although healing was slow, it came. Twelve years later, Shaela still has some nightmares, momentary flashbacks, and brief pangs of guilt. But in His faithfulness, He has healed her scars and given her an abundant life.

Unlike Ichabod's mother, Shaela has allowed God to birth joy in her.

I can testify to the fact that Shaela glorifies God and trusts Him fully. She radiates peace and selflessness. It is evident that Jesus is her all in all, and that He has done a miraculous work in her life. And she blesses others with her compassion and enthusiasm for life. Though she has been through dark times since the shooting, God has sustained and provided for her, sometimes in miraculous ways.

She notes, "Jeremiah 29:11 says that He knows the plans He has for His children; plans to give us a hope and a future. Even now, when my circumstances seem to crush me, He brings this truth to my mind and I am filled with joy—trusting that He is faithfully shaping me into the woman He desires me to be."

Sister, no matter your situation, God wants to come near to you. He longs to give you the peace and strength you need to persevere.

The question is, will you show up—not give up?

Remember that He always shows up for *us*. Even when we don't feel Him there, He is present. Oh, how I pray that we will be women who believe that God has a plan; that He hasn't left just because we sometimes don't see or feel Him. I encourage you to latch on to Him. Lean hard into His comfort . . . and receive the supernatural peace only He can give.

Press on and receive the only prize worth striving for: Jesus.

11

Jephthah's Daughter
From Healthy to Hurt

✳ JUDGES 11 ✳

TINA ✳ His strong arms thrust me upward and I landed on his broad shoulders. My hands nervously dug into the top of his head while my scrawny legs dangled around his neck.

"Don't let go, Daddy!" I said, trying to get my balance.

"I won't. I have you." He held tight to my limbs, which gave me courage to ease the grip on his head.

"Now reach up and grab hold of the bulb," he said.

"I'm scared!" I cried. To a young girl's eyes, it appeared as if I were as high as a mountain.

"You're all right," he soothed.

I reached way out and stretched my small frame to the height of the tall ceiling. My body lifted off his shoulders. He tightened his grip on my legs, pulling them deeper into his chest. With every turn of the bulb, my body shifted. One hand remained clamped to his head while the other trembled as it unscrewed the lightbulb. Though I was scared, in my small mind I understood my father's strength and knew he would not drop me. In those few moments, I felt safe and secure.

I wish I could say my perception of my father being a great warrior, one who could hold me up during my most difficult times in life, remained strong—but it did not.

A Soldier's Daughter

Little girls look upon their fathers as heroes and soldiers of all kinds. To them, their father can conquer the most dangerous enemies, evict the ghosts beneath their beds, and raise them up with the strongest of arms. Jephthah's daughter thought so as well. Though her name is not recorded, her opinion of her father was clear. She loved her daddy.

Jephthah was born out of wedlock, to a prostitute. Raised by his dad and stepmother, who also had sons, the boys grew through childhood and adolescence. Closer to adulthood, the half brothers "drove Jephthah away" and told him he would never receive any inheritance because he was "the son of another woman" (Judg. 11:2).

What a hurtful moment. We can imagine how wounded Jephthah must have felt when he was isolated from his family and stripped of his home and inheritance. Jephthah finally settled in the land of Tob, where other men began to follow him. In spite of (a friend of mine would say, "because of") Jephthah's past, he somehow had become a faithful believer in the one true God. And when his name was spoken, others knew that he was a "mighty warrior" (v. 1).

At some point, war broke out between the Ammonites and the Gileadites, which led the elders of Gilead to find Jephthah. They asked him to come back and serve as commanding officer to the army. Jephthah agreed, not realizing the impact his decision would have on his relationship with his only daughter.

After Jephthah became commander of the Gileadites, he immediately sent a message to the Ammonite king, asking him to stand down.

After their correspondence, it became clear the king would continue with the war.

During the battle, the Spirit of the Lord came upon Jephthah, and his army was able to advance against the Ammonites (v. 29). Jephthah rose up before his men. With all of his strength, he shouted out to God: "If you give the Ammonites into my hands, whatever comes out of the door of my house to meet me when I return in triumph from the Ammonites will be the LORD's, and I will sacrifice it as a burnt offering" (vv. 30–31).

It's impossible to comprehend Jephthah's hasty vow to the Lord. How could he publicly proclaim he would sacrifice the first thing that exited his doors to greet him? What was he thinking? Did it not occur to him that it could be someone he cared for? Jephthah was willing to do anything to secure his victory, and in the end, the Lord granted his request. "When Jephthah returned to his home in Mizpah, who should come out to meet him but his daughter, dancing to the sound of timbrels! She was an only child" and the first one out the door (v. 34).

A Daughter's Wound

"When [Jephthah] saw her, he tore his clothes and cried, 'Oh no, my daughter! You have brought me down and I am devastated. I have made a vow to the LORD that I cannot break'" (v. 35).

Imagine the girl's excitement as she flung open the doors and headed straight for her dad. She expected a wonderful reunion, seeing her father return after a long, fearful absence. Customary for that time period, the servants of the household grabbed their tambourines and celebrated his victory. However, Jephthah's daughter ran ahead of the servants. She wanted to be the first to greet her father. As she ran to embrace him, she had no idea of the ache in his heart. Rather than being received by his warm embrace, she saw him raise his arms to his chest to forcefully rip his clothing, an act that symbolized grief and a period of mourning.

I'm sure concern replaced her joyous jubilance. She had no idea what Jephthah meant. The impact of her wound came after her father's explanation: "You have brought me down and I am devastated."

What could Jephthah's daughter have thought? *What did I do?* "I'm sorry . . . I didn't know." Like a scolded child, confusion fell on her face as she tried to make sense of it all.

Jephthah told his daughter the tragedy was her doing. "You have brought me down. You did this to me. You completely destroyed me!" Rather than Jephthah taking full responsibility for his own actions, he pushed the issue on his daughter and made her responsible.

As a little girl, I remember a horrific moment: the only time my father ever hit me. I was the ninth child out of twelve kids. (Yes, all from one mom and dad.) My father drank heavily in my younger years, and this was one of those times. My sister and I asked him to put Christmas lights on some wood that outlined the shape of a cross and place the cross in our front yard. We were so excited. We stood at the front door and watched the lights twinkle on and off.

Suddenly things changed. My father rushed into the house and—without warning—slapped me across the face so hard that I stumbled over a chair behind me. I was completely caught off guard. Devastated and humiliated in front of my family, I stood frozen, tears streaming down my cheeks. Upon further investigation, I learned that because I was standing next to the light switch in the doorway, my father thought I was turning the light switch on and off, making the lights blink. He quickly learned that the Christmas lights were the kind that twinkled on and off by themselves. In the midst of his sorrow, he spent many days trying to make it up to me.

And though Jephthah did not physically hit his daughter, the alarm she felt at his actions may have felt similar.

"I have made a vow to the LORD that I cannot break" (v. 35). Jephthah poured his heart out in explanation to his daughter. What a painful moment between the two of them! Envision the impact of those words, the surprise of what her father spoke. What feelings gripped her? What misery ran through her soul? How deeply did she suffer? Did she receive the responsibility for what had happened, or did the situation immediately change her view of her father? The wound was overwhelming.

Do you remember a time when you felt the sting of disappointment concerning your father? That moment you realized your father was not Superman, not perfect? That your father might have made a mistake? Or perhaps it was a moment your father blamed you for something. Suddenly things between you changed as your view of him changed. It's painful. The wound can bring such a burst of pain to the strings attached to our hearts—especially the one that has our father's name on it.

I am amazed at Jephthah's daughter. Because her father loved God, she more than likely had a love for God as well. Yes, Jephthah made a hasty vow. Yes, Jephthah arrogantly boasted. Yes, he blamed his daughter for his wrongdoing. Yet, with all she experienced in that traumatic moment, she did not rise up in anger against her father. She didn't defend herself either. She simply submitted to the authority of her father and his vow to the Lord.

When our fathers say and do things that hurt us, how will we respond?

> "My father," she replied, "you have given your word to the Lord. Do to me just as you promised, now that the Lord has avenged you of your enemies, the Ammonites. But grant me this one request," she said. "Give me two months to roam the hills and weep with my friends, because I will never marry." (vv. 36–37)

Sometimes we hold a wound in the palm of our hands and have no idea what to do with it. Everyone's healing will look different. Some women need counseling to get through the hurt; others will spend many nights on their knees in prayer. Some women need to talk—a lot—until the wound subsides. And others will need to process it internally and quietly. Understanding exactly what she needed, Jephthah's daughter chose to go away for a while and grieve with her friends.

The Bible clearly states that Jephthah said, "whatever comes out of the door of my house to meet me . . . I will sacrifice it as a burnt offering," and some scholars believe that because he was raised a Gilead, whose worship rituals involved child and human sacrifice, he would indeed literally do as he stated. Furthermore, the Mosaic Law says that if you make a vow to the Lord, don't be slow to pay it (Deut. 23:21–23). Many people believe the Scripture to mean what it says, and that Jephthah did sacrifice his daughter.

Other scholars do not believe that he meant to literally sacrifice his daughter on an altar. According to Mosaic Law, God forbade human offerings. If Jephthah was truly a man who honored God, he would have honored God's law. Many believe that the Scripture implies that the sacrifice was for Jephthah's daughter to remain celibate throughout her life. She would never marry or bear children—thus the explanation of verses 37 and 39, which indicate that she was a virgin and would remain so. With her friends at her side, Jephthah's daughter mourned the loss of not being able to marry. She mourned the loss of not being able to have children. And she mourned the loss of not being able to carry on her family name and heritage. Such a future, in itself, was death.

Whatever the final outcome of this scene, it was a horrendous wound.

Heartbreaker to Heart Builder

As the days continued, I looked at the man who once held a little girl high upon his strong shoulders and wondered where the soldier had gone. As I matured, my knowledge and understanding matured. I came to see my father as a human being with many flaws. His imperfections became more evident, often outweighing his good qualities. Sin played a huge role in that, encasing everything wonderful about him. Like a cocoon, the sin in my father's life kept the good hidden, leaving us to view the ugly in him—instead of the glory. The sin left our hearts broken in a million pieces, longing for the father we wished we'd had. Over time, something within me clicked. I realized that my earthly father could not save me, or the world. I realized my father could not even save himself; only God could do that.

The Lord opened my eyes to see that sometimes fathers hurt their children. Often, children have huge expectations of their fathers. But if we put someone on a pedestal, they will eventually fall. We often look closely at the one who has fallen, rather than the one who placed them on the pedestal to begin with.

I finally realized that God had the power to control, fix, and work in all things. I did not. I realized that God, not my earthly father, was the ruler of the world. From that moment on, I also realized that the one perfect father, whom I could look up to, was my heavenly Father.

Friends, I ache with all of you who've had a terrible father at some point in your life. A father who never rose to the occasion to take care of the beautiful gift God gave him when He gave him *you*. A father who was a heartbreaker instead of a heart builder, who had no idea what to say to a little girl desperately longing for a father's attention. A father who neglected to teach his daughter how to recognize a godly man who would treat her the way she should be treated. Daughters everywhere are thirsting for and desiring a father who will love and protect and cherish them! Sadly, many are left to fill the void in other ways.

Precious daughter of Christ, do not lose hope. There is someone who can provide you with everything you long for! He is the builder of hearts and the restorer of our souls. He is the most perfect Father we could ever wish for. He is the One we can always turn to, whether or not we're in a good relationship with our earthly father.

Later on, my father gave up drinking and came to know the same heavenly Father I fell in love with. My Father became his Father. What a glorious moment for both of us! After a continuous work of healing, I saw a gentle, caring, and affectionate father, and I began to love him even more. My prayer is that you will see those kinds of changes in your father too.

In the meantime, let us grab hold of what the psalmist proclaimed: "I will proclaim the LORD's decree: He said to me, 'You are my son; today I have become your father'" (Ps. 2:7). May that become our boast as well!

DENA ❦ Nikole Hahn's story is one of family and father-wounds healed through God's grace. She says, "My healing began the moment I walked away from the toxic relationships in my family. Growing up, I felt so misunderstood and helpless, with a vague feeling of not being accepted and that something was wrong. When I married, I tried earning my family's love, putting my marriage in jeopardy until the truth could not be denied. I had to walk away to save me, to have a closer relationship with God, and to salvage my marriage."

Like Jephthah's daughter, Nikole took time to grieve. The loss of familial relationships wounded her deeply. Even though she knew it was the right decision, after severing ties with her family, she suffered several months of deep depression. In the midst of her pain, Nikole read the Bible and prayed constantly, until one day she realized she had to "leave the couch and get back to living again. I remembered something precious in Sheila Walsh's book, *The Heartache No One Sees*. She said to pray for those that hurt you—even if you are gritting your teeth in the beginning. Eventually, you'll mean it."

God has taught Nikole much: "The first time I saw them, I thought I had forgiven them, but I felt only anger. A year later, seeing them again brought pity. I rejoiced in that, because I knew I had finally forgiven them. It had taken me two years to finally work through a lifetime of anger over my childhood 'daddy issues.'"

Nikole explains that her healing process wasn't without its ups and downs. "Every time I saw them in town, my nightmares would return," she says. "But lately, those have stopped too. I don't sleepwalk anymore. I have lost forty-five pounds, and my faith has strengthened. I have seen God work in the last several years in both supernatural and practical ways. I still work at calling him 'Father'; some of my prayers begin with *Dear Lord* or *Dear God.*"

Healing and forgiveness began with Nikole's praying for her family, or her "enemy." The Bible states in Matthew 5:43–48 that to love a friend is easy, but to love your enemy is far more difficult. Says Nikole, "The Scriptures are right. The benefits outweigh the pain! My Bible is open more often, and I have become a prayer warrior through God's redemption of my pain."

Father to the Fatherless

Do you have "daddy issues," as Nikole did? Perhaps, like Tina, your father was abusive. Did he grieve you by blaming you for something he should have taken responsibility for, like Jephthah did to his daughter? Maybe he was distant or your mother raised you alone. Each kind of father-wound is debilitating in its own way.

Did you know that God has a special place in His heart for those who have no fathers or have been wounded by their earthly dads? The term "fatherless" appears repeatedly in Scripture. Over and over in the Bible, God links widows, foreigners, and outcasts with those who have no fathers. And His idea of justice always includes taking care of those without dads.

Psalm 68:5 notes, "A father to the fatherless, a defender of widows, is God in his holy dwelling." And Psalm 146:9 says, "The LORD watches over the foreigner and sustains the fatherless and the widow, but he frustrates the ways of the wicked."

Mary DeMuth is a Christian author and speaker who endured childhood abuse and now encourages men and women to "live uncaged" through the power of Jesus. Her father died when she was ten, leaving her with a mother who struggled with addiction and often left Mary alone or with abusive people. "It isn't easy to be a fatherless girl," she admits.

In a beautiful blog post she penned after attending a funeral for a friend's father, she wrote:

> [My father] didn't live to see awkward me in junior high, hugging the walls of my cafeteria, waiting for boys to ask me to dance. (They didn't.) He didn't read my suicide poetry. Didn't rejoice when I met Jesus at fifteen. Didn't see me graduate high school or college. Didn't walk me down the aisle. Didn't hold his grandchildren. Didn't give sage advice about being grown up. He, the overly gifted author, never held one of my books in his hands.
>
> On this Memorial Day, I remember my flawed, messy father. I miss him. And a little of me still mourns.
>
> And in that broken place, oh how it breaks afresh, I reach for my Father's hand. The One who never leaves. The One who stood by me at dances, who lamented my suicidal thoughts. The One who nabbed me from this crazy world at fifteen and chose me for His kingdom. The One who gave me gumption to graduate and succeed. The One who healed my broken heart enough to entrust myself to marriage. The One who parented me well so I could parent my children. The One who gave me a grace-filled, outrageously miraculous life—one worthy of writing about. The One who penned stories through me.
>
> I celebrate my father and my Father today. Bittersweet and beautiful.[1]

1. Mary DeMuth, "Losing a Father," *Mary DeMuth, Live Uncaged* (blog), May 26, 2012, http://www.marydemuth.com/2012/05/losing-a-fathe/

Broken to Beautiful

As Tina noted, God is the only perfect Father. And He longs to take you in His arms, where you can rest and be restored. When our daddies break our hearts, Jesus rebuilds them.

Unlike Jephthah's daughter, you don't have to grieve without hope. Instead, you can work through the pain caused by an imperfect father, with God's help. Dear one, He can do for you what He did for Mary and for Nikole. Only the Creator of the universe has the power to heal our brokenness—and rewrite our stories.

The question is: will we say yes to Him? Will we let Him hold the pen and be the Author of our days? Or will we try to wrestle the pen from Him and create a future that we want, no matter the consequences?

It's so tempting to hold on to our hurts, nurture our grudges, and feed our resentment. Many of us feel as if we didn't get what we deserved as children, and we blame God for it. Blame Him for not coming to our rescue. Do you think He doesn't see your pain? That He still isn't coming to your rescue? Are your wounds deep enough that you believe you'll never feel peace?

If so, God wants to re-create your image of Him . . . and of yourself. He desires that you be whole and holy. He wants to dress you in pure, white robes, put a crown on your head, and help you claim your godly inheritance, which Jesus Christ earned for you through His death and resurrection. You are a dazzling, royal princess in His kingdom!

I love what speaker and author Sheri Rose Shepherd posted on Facebook when I was writing this chapter: "What you may see as broken inside yourself, your Father sees as beautiful. He is the one who makes beautiful things out of broken hearts. He is the same God who took a brokenhearted orphan named Esther and turned her into a queen who saved her people. He loves you, and He will not waste a single tear you have shed."

My relationship to my own father has been a work-in-progress. We

were, and are, very different people, and his struggles with his temper
when I was a child confused, angered, and hurt me.

But God is a mighty Healer, and I can testify that when we give Him
our hurts, He gently tends them. Jesus, in His merciful grace, gives us
the medicine we need, as only the Great Physician can.

Lunch with Dad

"Can I take you to lunch?" Dad asks. "Your mom has an art class, and
I'm driving over with her."

I look down at my calendar, which is unusually bare today.

"I'd love it," I say, and we make plans for him to pick me up later.

He hugs me when we see each other and asks me where I'd like to
eat. We choose a healthy café downtown, and after we're seated, he
folds his hands to pray for us.

Suddenly, I have a lump in my throat.

I think of him a few months ago, with ash-gray skin and breathing by
machine. His triple bypass happened unexpectedly, and I was grateful
my family and I had moved to the city where his surgery occurred—an
hour from the ranch he and Mom live on—the year before.

In the cold, sterile pre-op room, my brother, Mom, and I held hands
with him and prayed, while he tried not to cry. It's hard to see your
daddy tear up. And harder still to say good-bye, not knowing if it's the
last one.

Thankfully, his operation was successful, though he stayed in a
rehab facility for several weeks. During his arduous recovery, I was able
to visit him regularly.

"Amen," Dad says, and I echo his words as we pick up the menus.
When we order soup and salad, he harasses the server, which normally
embarrasses me. This time, though, I just smile.

We talk of everything—and nothing. I tell him about a friend's
messy divorce, and ask his professional opinion about whether or not
the legal advice she got was correct. He asks me about my husband's

job search, and my new boss. And when he offers to buy dessert, I don't wave him off. We linger over coffee and chocolate.

For years after I left home, I wrestled with the way Dad raised my brother and me. We lived twenty miles from town, and I often felt isolated and lonely. He wasn't much for socializing, and I resented him for keeping people away. I also felt smothered by a strict upbringing. And during the first decade of my life, an anger problem kept Dad chained and the rest of us unsettled.

But over time, I learned a bit about his childhood and young adult years, which had been traumatic. I sought counseling for anxiety and perfectionist tendencies, and learned more about the perfect Father who had given me my family. And gradually, the expectations and frustrations that had hardened my heart toward Dad faded away. As I had children of my own, I recognized the Herculean job God gives parents, and I forgave my mother and father for their failings.

I also began to count the blessings in my relationship with Dad. Unlike many daughters, I never once doubted that my earthly father loved me . . . even if he sometimes had funny ways of saying it ("Have you checked your oil lately?"). He provided well for our family, so Mom could stay at home. She shopped, cleaned, sewed, cooked dinner every night, and fully supported my Dad in his part-time music ministry— giving me both stability and a godly role model to emulate. As a successful small-business owner who began as a poor son of cotton pickers, he taught me hard work, discipline, and perseverance, and those traits have served me well in my career as an author. He also supported my dreams and goals. Most important, Dad has never failed to express pride in having me as a child.

And through the years, Dad allowed God to soften his sharp edges. Now, with my two boys, he's kind, patient, and funny. He apologizes when he messes up, and is quick with hugs and kisses. And I know from experience that if I ever need prayers, a loan, or a listening ear, Dad is more than happy to oblige.

God has sewn grace into both our hearts. For that—and the gift of more time with my dad—I'm unspeakably grateful.

When he takes me back to work, I thank him for making time for me. "Wouldn't miss it," he says.

I feel the same way.

Finding Our True Home

Daughter of heaven, He sees your pain. He knows that you are tired of crying, weary of trying. And He wants to be your protector, rescuer, and provider. Unlike our earthly fathers, he cannot fail you, because He is God. He will not leave you, because He can't break His promises. Isaiah 30:18 says, "Yet the LORD longs to be gracious to you; therefore he will rise up to show you compassion. For the LORD is a God of justice. Blessed are all who wait for him!" And Psalm 10:14 says, "But you, God, see the trouble of the afflicted; you consider their grief and take it in hand. The victims commit themselves to you; you are the helper of the fatherless."

Maybe you feel too weak to take the first step toward healing. Surely, Jephthah's daughter felt shaken to her core when she heard the unthinkable promise her father made. Like this Old Testament figure, has your father's sin pinned you to the floor, and you can't move? Has he wounded you so deeply that you can't imagine ever speaking to him again, let alone forgiving him or getting past your pain?

If so, let the words of this passage wash over you like blessed, life-giving rain:

> But he said to me, "My grace is sufficient for you, for my power is made perfect in weakness." Therefore I will boast all the more gladly of my weaknesses, so that the power of Christ may rest upon me. For the sake of Christ, then, I am content with weaknesses, insults, hardships, persecutions, and calamities. For when I am weak, then I am strong." (2 Cor. 12:9–10 ESV)

If you ask Jesus, He will be your strength. I know this for sure, because for over thirty-five years—through illness, pain, miscarriage, depression, parenting and marriage challenges, betrayal, persecution, and loneliness—He has been mine.

Meditate on Psalm 23 from *The Message*, allowing its familiar comfort in unfamiliar phrasing to speak to your heart:

> GOD, my shepherd!
>   I don't need a thing.
> You have bedded me down in lush meadows,
>   you find me quiet pools to drink from.
> True to your word,
>   you let me catch my breath
>   and send me in the right direction.
>
> Even when the way goes through
>   Death Valley,
> I'm not afraid
>   when you walk at my side.
> Your trusty shepherd's crook
>   makes me feel secure.
>
> You serve me a six-course dinner
>   right in front of my enemies.
> You revive my drooping head;
>   my cup brims with blessing.
>
> Your beauty and love chase after me
>   every day of my life.
> I'm back home in the house of God
>   for the rest of my life.

That well-loved psalm conjures up images of rest, peace, and relief. As someone who's moved quite a bit in her adult life, it makes me think of a gracious, comfortable home where I can put my stuff in the cabinets and closets and spread out—knowing I'll be there awhile.

Like many people do, I used to see God as a parent who wanted to punish me when I was "bad" and who waited for me to mess up. However, after walking with Him and experiencing His grace, I now know God as the nurturing Father who gently tucks me into green meadows when I'm tired, gives me a drink of Living Water when I'm thirsty, feeds me with the Bread of Life when I'm hungry, holds my hand when I'm scared, and fights off my enemies with His weapons.

Sisters, He is our true home, the only home that will never be torn away from us. No matter what we've done, or what others have done to us, we can always come back to Him. And when we do, we'll discover that His beauty and love have been chasing after us the whole time.

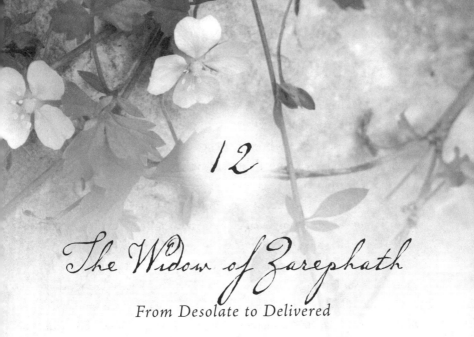

12

The Widow of Zarephath

From Desolate to Delivered

❧ 1 Kings 17 ❧

TINA ❧ Two teens were carried out to sea by a strong current off the South Carolina coast. For six days, they drifted alone in the vast ocean. With cracked, dry lips scorched from the sun, they were in dire need of food and water. To add to it, the freezing nights left them in despair. At one point a large ship crossed their path, but due to the size of the boat, no one noticed the boys were even there. The large ship passed right by them. The teens lost all hope, and wanting to end their suffering, they contemplated suicide.

The next day, night fell and the stars glistened above them as they continued to drift. Suddenly a light came from the dark waters. Jelly balls, they called them, floated up to the boat. One of the teens grabbed hold of one and bit into it, hoping the jelly ball would either kill him or satisfy his hunger. Well, it didn't kill him, and may have satisfied him in some way.[1] Little did the teens know, God brought food right up to

1. "The cannonball [jellyfish] has great potential value as a food item in the world

their boat. Perhaps they couldn't recognize it as such because it wasn't in the way they expected.

At their lowest point, the boys scratched out a note to their loved ones as their final good-bye. With all hope lost, their weak bodies lay lifeless in the boat, waiting to die. And in their greatest moment of despair, in the dreary stillness, they heard something: an engine. Suddenly their eyes fell upon a huge fishing boat coming toward them. As their hearts raced, they understood one thing: help was on the way!

As I watched the show and read about the boys and their survival,[2] I noticed several things. In the center of their terrible situation, they prayed and talked to God. They also sang and worshipped God, even while suffering. The most amazing insight was seeing how God made possible what seemed impossible—He rescued them.

Sometimes our lives feel as if we are surrounded by a vast ocean and it's too difficult to find our way out. The burden feels just as deep and wide as any ocean. We float along like a loose raft, carried away by the strength of the tide. Many folks are faced with foreclosure, bills they have no way to pay, or a business barely making it. Families struggle to put food on the table. Some are torn apart by a parent needing to work in another state. Do you relate? If so, you're not alone in your suffering. Many others have found themselves in

---

market. The most important fact about the protein in the cannonball jellyfish is the collagen it contains. Our bodies need collagen to build cell tissue, cartilage, teeth and bones. Scientific research continues on collagen and its medical potential. For over a thousand years, Asians have been eating jellyfish for medicinal reasons to treat high blood pressure, arthritis, bronchitis and other diseases. The cannonball jellyfish is an ideal diet food because it is low in fat, cholesterol and calories." FoodReference.com, accessed April 11, 2013, http://www.foodreference.com/html/art-jellyfish-7806.html.

2. See Associated Press, "Two Teens Rescued after 6 Days Adrift," NBCnews.com, May 3, 2005, http://www.msnbc.msn.com/id/7706851/ns/us_usnews/t/two-teens-rescued-after-days-adrift/; and "Boys Adrift," *I Shouldn't Be Alive*, season 3, episode 5, Discovery Channel, January 22, 2010.

crucial circumstances. It's a devastating wound that pierces the heart as deeply as any other.

A Widow's Wound

Zarephath is a Sidonian or Phoenician city on the Mediterranean coast. Sarafand, as it is called today, is located in Lebanon about thirteen miles north of Tyre. At the time the widow lived, there was a great famine. The Bible doesn't speak of what happened to the widow's husband, but we can assume that her husband died in the famine. The widow was now left to care for herself as well as their son. With no possibility of producing crops and animals moving to greener pastures, food became scarce. Suddenly, the widow's dire circumstances placed her in a terrible situation—creating an unbearable wound.

Heavy-laden and burdened, she bent over to pick up a piece of dead wood. Her eyes swept across the barren, cracked land to find another. It had not rained for over three years. As she took several more steps on the hard earth, dust rose up and clung to her dirty feet. Her weak body turned, and she grabbed at another twig. Because her thoughts lay elsewhere, she did not notice the man walking toward the city gate.

"Would you bring me a little water in a jar so I may have a drink?" Elijah called out to her.

Weak and too depressed to say a word, she simply left to get the water.

"And bring me, please, a piece of bread," he added.

Stunned by his request, she turned and replied, "As surely as the LORD your God lives . . . I don't have any bread—only a handful of flour in a jar and a little olive oil in a jug."

With heartbreak etched on her face, she continued, "I am gathering a few sticks to take home and make a meal for myself and my son, that we may eat it—and die" (1 Kings 17:10–12).

Was that her solution—death? In her suffering and desperate need, she couldn't see that there might be any other way out of her circumstances. The reality was that she and her son would die, because they were about to eat the last of their food.

Elijah must have noticed her emotions. This man of God traveled through the wasteland. He understood the drought. He understood her place of complete and utter brokenness. He also understood that God sent him to her, and that God chose this woman to help Elijah.

Thick emotion hung in the air.

Elijah stepped closer to the widow. He, too, was tired and worn from his travels. Settled beneath the wings of his Lord, he gently spoke, "Don't be afraid" (v. 13).

At those words, my emotions would have spilled over: "Don't be afraid." How many times in our distress have we longed for someone to speak that phrase to us? Elijah was a prophet of the Lord and could discern her fear and hopelessness.

The Bible doesn't tell how she responded when Elijah expressed those words, but let us imagine. Was she in such despair she couldn't cry? Or did long-buried emotions come flooding forth? Whatever her reaction, she stood in the stillness without whispering a word. "Go home and do as you have said. But first make a small loaf of bread for me from what you have and bring it to me, and then make something for yourself and your son" (v. 13). Any normal mother would fight back or raise her voice against such an insane command. She would have guarded what little food she had left. But there was simply no fight left in her—she had given up. She didn't know anything about this man who stumbled into her broken world, who now stood before her, asking her to prepare him a meal with the last of her food.

A stillness must have settled on the two of them as Elijah gently said, "For this is what the LORD, the God of Israel, says: 'The jar of flour will not be used up and the jug of oil will not run dry until the day the LORD sends rain on the land'" (v. 14). Without saying a word, the widow turned to obey Elijah's request.

For each of us, there will be a moment God speaks—through His

Word or through someone else. He will send us help and hope. He will give us a choice to either move forward or stay sunken in our great despair. The widow chose to obey Elijah. Because of her obedience, "there was food every day for Elijah and for the widow and her family. For the jar of flour was not used up and the jug of oil did not run dry, in keeping with the word of the LORD spoken by Elijah" (vv. 15–16).

There are wounds we will face due to our circumstances. We will feel like the widow of Zarephath—despairing and defeated. But hope is waiting. God is waiting.

The Potter Feeds

In desperate situations, God feeds His children. Will we be able to recognize the feeding? What will it look like? God not only fed the widow and her son, but he also fed Elijah. When Elijah found himself under a broom tree wanting to die, God sent an angel to feed him. When the disciples wanted to send five thousand people away, God fed them. When the Israelites complained about their desperate situation in the desert, God sent manna and fed them. Hiding from Saul who wanted to kill him, David sent his men to Nabal's house for food, and God fed them through Abigail.

During desperate times, God is still working, teaching, and taking care of us. Can we draw close to God, trusting He is sculpting and shaping us, like the great potter He is? Trusting that through our trials and tribulation, He is building character, strengthening our weaknesses, and revealing Himself? Though we feel the deep impressions of His hand, can we trust that in the end He is creating a masterpiece?

When a potter creates, he will often pull the clay toward him to maneuver the clay into the perfect shape he is looking for. Each vessel is unique; crafted in its own special way. That's what God does with us in our wounded situation; He pulls us toward Himself, while crafting us into perfection. Of course, we can fight every move God tries to make in our life, but wouldn't that get tiring?

The widow of Zarephath could have completely ignored Elijah's request and walked away, leaving herself to wallow in her wound, but she didn't. Instead, she yielded to the helper God had sent and honored his request.

Later on in the chapter, the widow's son died—another wound. The woman thought perhaps his death was due to her own sin, but it was not. Elijah prayed, "LORD my God, let this boy's life return to him!"—and her son was brought back to life (v. 21). Through that situation, the widow finally acknowledged: "Now I know that you are a man of God [here's the best part] and that the word of the LORD from your mouth is the truth" (v. 24). God sent Elijah to feed her not only physically but also emotionally and spiritually. God brought life into her empty vessel.

So how do we live, breathe, and survive in our difficult circumstances? Paul seemed to have the answer:

> I rejoiced greatly in the Lord that at last you renewed your concern for me. Indeed, you were concerned, but you had no opportunity to show it. I am not saying this because I am in need, for I have learned to be content whatever the circumstances. I know what it is to be in need, and I know what it is to have plenty. I have learned the secret of being content in any and every situation, whether well fed or hungry, whether living in plenty or in want. I can do all this through him who gives me strength. (Phil. 4:10–13)

God promised in Isaiah 41:10, "So do not fear, for I am with you; do not be dismayed, for I am your God. I will strengthen you and help you; I will uphold you with my righteous right hand." It is a promise I want to hold on to—that God *will* help me, no matter what I'm facing. And though I'm an unworthy piece of clay which He holds in His right hand, through my circumstances, He will shape me into something wonderful.

Our circumstances are not always what we would choose. At times, they will seem desperate, and we will feel defeated. The question is, will we be able to draw near to God in the midst of them? Will we allow God to comfort us through them? What hope can we hold on to? Will we allow God to feed us in the way He chooses? Can we change our *defeated* into *delivered*?

While working at a retirement center two days a week as a music therapist, I made a glorious friend. "Heinz" shuffled his feet and blew out short breaths of air as he made his way to the chair beside me. He came early to every session. On one particular day, we had an opportunity to visit more than usual. As he spoke, I glanced above his ear where a hearing aid was transplanted into the side of his head. He had lost his hearing from a beating he'd endured in a concentration camp.

"Heinz, do you mind telling the story about your days in the camp?" I asked.

His thick accent carried me back to the scene. He shared about sleeping on the cold floors in the dead of winter with no blanket or anything to keep his feet warm.

"They beat us every day," he said. "And we had no food—we were starving." I couldn't imagine the suffering. Heinz was only twenty-one at the time of his captivity, separated from his family who thought he was dead. One day, he saw a dust storm rising in the distance. He stopped, stared, and declared to himself, "If the storm comes over the camp, I am going to escape." He waited, watched, and hoped. As time passed, the storm drew nearer, until it finally swirled into the camp.

When the thick haze settled over him, Heinz ran across the yard toward the fence. "The guards on the tower shot in my direction, but they could not see me," he said, his voice intensifying. "I ran fast, and they could not find me. I jumped on the fence and felt the bullets fly by my head, but none of them hit me. Their eyes were blinded and they could not see."

My heart beat fast and I leaned closer to Heinz. Like a movie, the story unfolded, and I was lost in the emotion. "I ran into the forest," he said. Heinz soon heard dogs trailing behind him and hid. "I never traveled by day—only at night."

"How did you survive?" I asked.

"I took the fruit from the trees."

Fruit?

He must have noticed the question mark on my face because he continued, "The trees were full of fruit. I ate all the fruit from the trees in the forest, and that is how I survived until I crossed the Austrian border."

In the midst of that horrible suffering, God fed one fearful young man who desperately wanted to live—with fruit off the trees. I almost cried right there. God truly does feed His children. Heinz made it safely across the border and was eventually reunited with his family.

Whatever your condition, situation, or wound, know that just like He did with the widow, my friend Heinz, and the two young teens in the boat, God will take care of you, in more ways than you can imagine. Determine to seek Him. He promises, "Call on me and come and pray to me, and I will listen to you. You will seek me and find me when you seek me with all your heart" (Jer. 29:12–13).

Whatever you're facing right now, step toward God; run toward Him. Like the widow of Zarephath, determine to obey what He asks of you. He will send help, He will feed you, and the wound will ease as you allow His righteous right hand to tenderly care for you.

DENA ❀ I've seen it firsthand, many times: God is "Jehovah Jireh," our Provider. Nothing is impossible with Him, and what we can see with our eyes is only one part of a larger story He's writing with our lives.

Almost twenty years ago, when my husband and I were first married, we lived in a tiny one-bedroom apartment in a seminary housing complex. Because we were preparing to enter full-time ministry together, Carey and I both worked part time and attended classes. We didn't have much money, but we were following God's call on our lives, and we trusted Him to take care of our needs.

One day, I looked into our small pantry and saw that our food supplies were running low. I opened the freezer and fridge. They too were perilously empty—and payday was still a day away. *We have a credit card for emergencies, but I don't want to use it,* I thought. *I do have all the ingredients for a casserole, except for one: cream of mushroom soup.*

Later that afternoon, I'd be able to pick up a bag of groceries at a food giveaway for seminary students, which was sponsored by the kind folks at a local church. I'd receive day-old bread, some fresh items, maybe pastries, but I'd never gotten soup in the distribution. So I prayed, "Lord, could you put a can of mushroom soup in the bag? Then I could make the casserole. Carey really likes it, and it would get us through until I get my paycheck."

To be honest, I wasn't sure what would happen.

A couple of hours later, I stood in line for the giveaway. After taking the brown paper bag, which was stapled shut, I decided to open it in the car. I held my breath while I ripped it open. And then, there it was— right on top: a can of cream of mushroom soup.

I smiled and wiped away tears. *Thank you, Lord,* I prayed over and over as I drove home.

Though I participated in the giveaway for several more months, I never received another can of soup. But it was there when I needed it most.

Countless other women have also seen God provide for and sustain them at their moments of great need. We're sharing just a few here, praying that their testimonies, like the story of the widow in Zarephath, will encourage you.

From Whom All Blessings Flow

Julie Cosgrove, like the widow, was left without a spouse, or a viable way to fully support herself. She says:

> With one thud, my life changed. My husband lay dead on the bathroom floor. As a freelance writer pursuing my dream because my spouse had finally landed a great paying job, I suddenly dangled above an abyss of financial peril. I had no children at home and was nowhere near 60, so I didn't qualify for widow's benefits. Years of unstable employment for us both had absorbed our savings. And after final costs and funeral expenses, his small life insurance policy would only provide income for a year at most.
>
> Two weeks after the funeral, our house went on the market. I had a massive estate sale to raise money. Besides, I knew I would be downsizing into a one-bedroom apartment. Still enveloped in the swirling numbness of early widowhood, I was turned down for job after job. I tried to keep writing, but I couldn't concentrate. My bank account kept dwindling. Prayer warrior friends put in overtime for me.
>
> Then, after four months, the house came under contract with the stipulation I pay over five thousand dollars in repairs. I moved to an apartment in the big city thirty miles away, but had to pay a year's lease up front since I was "self-employed." The amount I owed for the year was within pennies of the check I'd deposited from the sale of my husband's truck. My soul smiled. The sun was breaking through the clouds of my life. God would provide for this widow.
>
> Then I got the call. Two days before the house closing, the deal fell through. The buyers had been caught in tax fraud. Now I had a mortgage again, and two utility bills. I had to pay for a lawn service since I'd sold the lawn mower. In a scorching

Texas summer, I traveled back and forth three times a week, despite soaring gasoline prices, to water the grass so it looked green when everyone else's had turned brown. The AC had to run 24/7. Utility bills loomed.

Economic uncertainty pulled me down into a vortex of despair. I flooded my pillow at night in soft sobs as I prayed to God for some sign of relief, some direction to go, some evidence that He cared. I clung to Matthew 6:25—Don't be anxious about your life, what you shall eat, or drink, or about your body, what you shall wear. The last sinews of my faith whispered, "Believe."

One rainy day, which I praised God for (because it meant I wouldn't have to drive down to water the grass), I puddle-hopped to my mail slot. I slit the seal open and my knees buckled. It contained a cashier's check and a letter. A reader of my devotionals inherited a good sum of money. Convicted by Christ to tithe it to a worthy cause, she'd prayed for guidance. In her heart, she heard a quiet voice whisper my name. It was dollar for dollar the exact amount I had spent to date on repairs, expenses, and upkeep of the house.

Tears gushed down my cheeks just as the phone rang. My realtor giddily told me the house had sold—for real this time. My heart sang, "Praise God from whom all blessings flow."

A Van from God

Carolyn Counterman's world turned upside down by her family members' problems, as well as her own. She had had to resign from her job because she couldn't work and deal with post-traumatic stress disorder at the same time. She says, "We thought God would surely get us through—but then the family fell apart. My son went to prison. My daughter-in-law lost custody of the kids because of her drug use, and because she had covered up my son's crime."

Carolyn and her husband suddenly had four grandkids living with them. They wondered how they were going to feed, clothe, and transport the children to appointments and church.

"We didn't mind asking God for food. We even asked Him for clothes, though it made me a little uncomfortable," Carolyn says. "But when a woman suggested to me that we pray for a van, I balked. Sure, we were having to take two cars everywhere we went with the kids, and it was an inconvenience. However, I had been taught as a youngster not to ask God for material things. We had three cars already. One of them was not paid for, and another needed repairs, but we had them. This woman was insistent, though, that we pray for a van."

The couple didn't have anything to lose by asking, so they prayed for a van: "It wouldn't hurt our feelings if God said no, because we never expected Him to say yes."

Then things got worse. Carolyn's father, who lived with them, began to have major problems with his car, so he borrowed their slightly broken car. Without her husband's income, Carolyn's daughter-in-law lost her van because she couldn't pay for it. So her in-laws lent her another of their cars. Says Carolyn, "We were down to one unpaid-for car—and sharing a broken car with my dad. Then the call came, while I was standing in the middle of Wal-Mart looking at socks. Some old friends had seen me joke on Facebook about needing a van. They wanted to know if anyone had solved my transportation problem. I said no."

The friends told Carolyn they wanted to buy her a van. She was floored. "They apologized—actually apologized—that it was not new and not the model I wanted!" she says.

Her friends bought the family a van, paying the tax, title, and license fees. They transferred it into Carolyn's name and handed her the key.

She says, "God had said 'Yes!' when I expected Him to say no. With our family so messed up, I expected God to be displeased with us, but He decided to bless us instead. He gave our friends a heart for our family and the money to buy a van. I know that God is not short on cash, but I still get surprised when He spends it on me."

He's Our Provider

God is not short on cash, that's for sure. And He's not short on compassion for His children, either. Realtor, homeschooling mom, and author Terri Camp realized that when she was at her wit's end.

"Raising seven kids as a single mom was never easy, but it became especially difficult when my ex-husband lost his job and couldn't provide any financial support. I was making under thirteen hundred dollars a month, and my rent was fourteen hundred a month."

One day as Terri was leaving church, she went for a drive in her car, crying out to God. He said to her spirit, "I will do exceedingly, abundantly, beyond all you can ask or think." Not much later, a check arrived at Terri's church from an anonymous donor; it covered her family's expenses for an entire month.

Terri says, "A few more months went by, and bills piled up, food supplies got short, and there wasn't any money coming in. I filled out paperwork to get government assistance. I had a phone interview in which they told me I was approved. They were going to send me some paperwork in the mail. All I had to do was sign it, and I would begin getting food stamps."

Driving home from work, Terri began to cry. This was not the way she had envisioned her life. Suddenly a song began flooding her thoughts: "Jehovah Jireh, my provider, His grace is sufficient for me, for me, for me." First the song was in her thoughts; then she began singing along.

"The tears dried, and my heart was encouraged. I knew that God was my provider, not the government. When I arrived home, I opened my mail to find that a relative had sent me enough money to get through six weeks of living expenses!"

Terri had just passed her real estate exam and was on her way to becoming a real estate agent. She says, "I was scared of jumping, but God provided in a huge way for me. Funny thing, the paperwork for the government assistance never did arrive in my mailbox."

Time after time, God provided more than enough for her and her family.

Nothing Is Impossible

I have experienced what Terri did. In explanation, let me tell you one more story.

Fourteen years after the cream of mushroom soup incident, my husband and I were taking a leap of faith. For eleven years, we'd been employed (Carey full-time, me part-time) in a Christian theater company. One or both of us had worked fifty weekends a year for more than a decade, and God was telling us it was time to do something else. The only problem? We weren't sure what the "something else" was.

We knew, however, that we needed to start fresh. After much prayer, we decided to sell our home and move to Amarillo, Texas, where my brother and his family lived. Amarillo was close to my parents, as well. Carey felt led to go back to graduate school and get another degree, so I prepared to work full-time for the first time in seven years.

Our house sold quickly, which was a miracle, since the economy was in a slump. However, after prepping my resume, scouting the paper, contacting everyone I knew, and applying for several jobs—with nothing to show for it—I began to get scared. Toward the end of June, when I couldn't sleep one night, I prayed, "Lord, I know you know this, but in three weeks, we're moving to a new city and neither of us will have a way to make money. I really need a job, and I trust you to provide that. But would you give me some guidance?"

Almost immediately, I thought of an online job board that I hadn't visited in a few weeks. Determined to check it when daylight came, I slept soundly. The next morning, I logged onto the board and saw the description of my dream job—one in which I could speak, write, network, and do public relations and media appearances for a nonprofit. I would be advocating for refugees who had been resettled after spending years in refugee camps. Several years before, I had felt impressed to learn and do more for the "least of these," and refugees certainly qualified.

I felt as if God had prepared me all my life for such a role.

After doing more research on the charity's website, I called the organization advertising the job and asked to speak to their human resources manager. Kelly was kind, and she encouraged me to apply immediately, because the board was in final interviews for the position. The job needed to be filled by the end of July because it was a grant-funded position and funding would begin August 1.

That day, I faxed my completed application, resume, and references to Catholic Charities of the Texas Panhandle. (I also prayed like crazy, and had all my friends pray, too!)

A week later, I underwent a telephone interview. Two weeks later, I flew up for an in-person interview, and a week after that, I was offered the job. Our last day of performances at the theater was July 20, 2010. My first day on the job as a community liaison for CCTP was July 26, 2010.

Carey and I didn't miss even one bill payment.

That isn't all. I found out later that another woman was almost hired to be the community liaison. However, Lori, the supervisor for that position, kept putting off the phone call to offer it to her. When she received my resume, Lori told Kelly that she didn't know what was going on: "Dena's resume is here, but she won't be in town for a few more weeks. We need to fill the position, but I just don't feel right about the person we've chosen, for some reason."

Kelly said, "Lori, you need to listen to that voice. God may be leading you in a different direction than what we originally thought." She encouraged Lori to call me, which she did. We hit it off immediately, and she decided that I was the right person for the job.

We serve a mighty God! Terri, Carolyn, and Julie found that out. In my own life, I've seen it many times. So has Tina. And the widow at Zarephath experienced it as well.

Tina and I pray that—however dire your current situation—you'll take God at His word. Remember what He promised us in the Sermon on the Mount?

> If you decide for God, living a life of God-worship, it follows that you don't fuss about what's on the table at mealtimes or whether the clothes in your closet are in fashion. There is far more to your life than the food you put in your stomach, more to your outer appearance than the clothes you hang on your body. Look at the birds, free and unfettered, not tied down to a job description, careless in the care of God. And you count far more to him than birds.
>
> Has anyone by fussing in front of the mirror ever gotten taller by so much as an inch? All this time and money wasted on fashion—do you think it makes that much difference? Instead of looking at the fashions, walk out into the fields and look at the wildflowers. They never primp or shop, but have you ever seen color and design quite like it? The ten best-dressed men and women in the country look shabby alongside them.
>
> If God gives such attention to the appearance of wildflowers—most of which are never even seen—don't you think he'll attend to you, take pride in you, do his best for you? What I'm trying to do here is to get you to relax, to not be so preoccupied with *getting*, so you can respond to God's *giving*. People who don't know God and the way he works fuss over these things, but you know both God and how he works. Steep your life in God-reality, God-initiative, God-provisions. Don't worry about missing out. You'll find all your everyday human concerns will be met." (Matt. 6:25–33 MSG)

We pray you'll remember that absolutely nothing is impossible with God. Just as He clothes the flowers of the field and feeds the birds of the air, He will feed, clothe, and shelter us.

Sister in Christ, the Author who's writing your life story can be fully trusted.

13

Conclusion

Hope for Shattered Hearts

As the lyrics of the old hymn "The Solid Rock" confirm:

> His oath, His covenant, His blood
> support me in the whelming flood.
> When all around my soul gives way,
> He then is all my hope and stay.
>
> On Christ, the solid Rock, I stand;
> all other ground is sinking sand.

Have you found that solid rock? We pray so . . . though we don't want to assume that everyone who reads this book has taken the step of making Jesus Christ her Lord and Savior. If you haven't, know that He loves you enough to die for you. He is wooing you, and longs for you to trust in Him.

TINA ✄ Are you to the place where you desire to hand over your wounds as well as your heart? Paul explains it so simply in Romans. He says "all have sinned and fall short of the glory of God" (3:23). "You see, at just the right time, when we were still powerless, Christ died for the ungodly" (5:6). He died so that we would *have* and *find* life.

And as we have encouraged you to express and share your wounds, let us also encourage you to share your decision with others, so you can find support and accountability. "If you declare with your mouth, 'Jesus is Lord,' and believe in your heart that God raised him from the dead, you will be saved. For it is with your heart that you believe and are justified, and it is with your mouth that you profess your faith and are saved" (10:9–10).

As we saw in the last chapter, God opened the widow of Zarephath's eyes so she could see Him in a new way. He desires that for us also. He wants to feed us and shepherd us.

At the time my brother was murdered, a group of men, also patients in the hospital, were putting together a large puzzle of the capital of Germany (where my brother had served in the army). Hours after his death, they decided, in honor of him, to finish the puzzle. It was a way they could find closure. They put the entire puzzle together, all but the last piece, which was missing. They stood back and stared at the puzzle, tears streaming down their cheeks. There *was* a piece missing— Michael—who was now with Jesus. They later put a picture of Michael where the missing piece of the puzzle was. The missing piece happened to be on the top of the puzzle in the clouds—in the heavens.

You see, God takes our wounds, the pieces of our life, and *He* puts the picture together. We see pieces of a puzzle, but God sees the big picture. We have difficulty finding the pieces and putting them where we think they should go, but God knows exactly where they should be. Sometimes our wounds leave us with missing pieces. And sometimes our wounds leave holes in our life's puzzle, but God comes in and fills the holes with a picture of Himself. God replaces the missing pieces with love, restoration, hope . . . and so much more. For some of us, God Himself is still the missing piece of the puzzle. My friends, we will never be able to make total sense of our lives, but we can trust that there is One who can.

Ruth never imagined God would lead her to a family who would introduce her to their God . . . ultimately placing her in the lineage of Christ. The widow of Zarephath had no idea God would send Elijah to help feed her physically and spiritually. Abigail could not see that her encounter with David would one day lead her to the palace as his wife. Ichabod's mother never dreamed God could use her son to change her family's legacy. Bathsheba never imagined she would endure such suffering but through it all, one day be crowned queen mother. Mary and Martha could not foresee Jesus raising their brother four days after he'd died. Just as He did for these biblical women, God is working in our often-puzzling lives. Trust Him, that in the midst of our wounded journeys, He knows where all the pieces fit.

DENA ❧ Maybe you trusted Jesus as your Savior when you were young. Perhaps you didn't follow Him, though—and you feel like you've messed up too much to come back to Jesus. If so, I want to "give the floor" to my friend Jennifer Ashley, so she can share her remarkable story.

> I became a Christian when I was eight years old, with little understanding of how to have a relationship with God. Throughout my young adult years, I engaged in rebellious activities. Despite my sin, though, God blessed me with many wonderful opportunities. But I rejected God, time after time. During my time of opportunity, I was dating Chris, who treated me with respect and selflessness. I became pregnant

outside of marriage in December 2001, and Chris and I decided to get married. But I simply didn't have the emotional capacity for that kind of relationship. Although he was good to me, I searched for something to heal my brokenness and insecurities. (I realize now that I was searching for Christ.)

Consequently, I became involved with a man who told me everything I wanted to hear. I cheated on my husband for years with this man, living in a web of lies. I eventually ended my marriage so that I could continue my relationship with him. And when our affair ended, I was devastated.

I had sacrificed many things to be with this man. I hurt people along the way, so many of my relationships were in need of extreme healing. Still, I didn't turn to God. In my mind, I had gone too far this time. I had blown it. I was dirty and wretched.

But I am convinced that God will go to the ends of the earth for those He calls His own. I was His, and I was at the end. On December 4, 2009, God reclaimed me.

Some newfound "friends" and I had volunteered to decorate a float for the annual Christmas parade of lights. It was bitterly cold, and we stayed warm by drinking liquor as we worked on the float. As the long day came to an end, I had my hands in my vest pocket and tried to jump over the trailer hitch. I didn't quite make it, and hit the ground face first.

I don't remember many of the details, but evidently, I got up and said that I was OK. The "friends" I was with became very afraid because this was a work function, and we had been drinking. They finally found one of my very best friends, Wendi, to take me with her. I am convinced that had they not found Wendi, they would have left me for dead in their car.

They told Wendi that I was drunk and had fallen, but failed to tell her the severity of my accident. Wendi took me on her float, and as I was riding through the parade, my life almost ended. Five things happened simultaneously; any one of them could have killed me: I had an insane amount of alcohol in my system, I had a severe concussion, I was hypothermic, I began having a seizure, and I completely stopped breathing.

When the paramedics arrived, they were unable to get anything down my throat to help me breathe, because I was seizing. Once I got to the emergency room, they were finally able to give me medication and place a tube down my throat.

After my friends called my parents and told them I was on life support, my folks rushed to the ER, where doctors said, "Mr. and Mrs. Salazar, we don't know how much brain damage your daughter is going to have. She was completely without oxygen for ten minutes, possibly more." My parents were devastated by this news.

But as God's grace would have it, after spending three days in ICU, I left the hospital without any permanent side effects or damage from the fall. I was perfectly fine! A few weeks later, I had a follow-up MRI on my brain. Technicians discovered that I had something called an AVM (arteriovenous malformation), which is simply an abnormal tangle of blood vessels. It was located in my right temporal lobe, behind my right eye, and could potentially cause brain bleeding. This didn't happen because of the fall; I had been born with the AVM. It was discovered because of the fall—and was potentially fatal.

All of this reminded me that even when we are not faithful, God is always faithful. It was as if everything rebellious, sinful, dark, and ugly hit the pavement with me on that frigid night in December.

I remember sitting in my room one evening, reading God's Word. A flood of guilt and shame rushed over me as I was reminded of all my bad choices.

And very sweetly, He spoke one word: "Praiseworthy."

Confused, I asked, "What?"

He said, "All of that is praiseworthy."

I said, "No, God, you don't understand. It's shameful, and it's ugly. My sin has changed the course of people's lives. I am worthless and I am dirty. My dearest friends hate me, and I deserve to be hated by them—by everybody."

He said, "Praiseworthy," again. As I tried to make sense of it, He spoke softly to me, "All of your rebellion, all of your bad choices, all of the darkest, deepest sin of your story is praiseworthy."

I asked Him how this could be possible. He said, "Because the life that you lived now honors and glorifies me. I gave you this story of how I love you and rescued you and it brings me honor and glory. Your story speaks of my perfect love, my sovereignty. You are the stage on which my power and glory is displayed. And it is praiseworthy."

God, in His unfailing love, made my rebellion and sinful nature praiseworthy! What a loving God!

The thought of my past life being praiseworthy is not easy to comprehend. It has taken longer than I expected to let go of my shame and guilt. And to be perfectly honest, I still struggle some days.

But in my quiet times, I hear God speak to my innermost being as He reveals His heart. When we focus on our sin, instead of His grace, it must feel like a slap in the face to God. He must say, "Why did I send my greatest sacrifice to suffer the worst possible death and to satisfy my wrath, if you hold on to what my Son already paid the highest price for?"

That fall allowed me to let go of my rebellion and run back to Christ. And you know what? He was running too. From there on, my days have been filled with gratitude and joy.

TINA & DENA ❧ Jennifer's story ended with her realization that God had been chasing her. Do you know, in the deepest part of your soul, that He pursues you too? That He took on hell and all its demons to woo you? That He loves you completely . . . irrevocably . . . even scandalously?

Oh, sister, it's true!

We pray you'll begin to let the truth of those words seep into your heart. Ruminate on them; pray about them; search the Scriptures for confirmation. It's all there.

Your wounds are real—but so is God's passion for you, His precious daughter.

What do we do with the hurts that have consumed so much of our lives? Our hope is that you will trudge through the mud, filth, and sludge to work through your wounds (as you do, know that we are so proud of you!). If you can strip away the hurtful layers and lay them at the feet of Jesus, it will be an amazing first step toward healing.

The "Talk It Out" sections of the study guide that follows are wonderful to use during girl times, friend gatherings, and/or Bible study moments. Our prayer is that if you've found healing from a wounded moment, you will lead, share, or facilitate "Talk It Out" sessions with other women. We learn so much from the experiences of others. And if you, my dear sister, are still carrying a wound, our "Write It Out" sections will enable you to go deeper and find much-needed healing.

We hope you will experience peace, assurance, and God's profound love during this process. We hope your eyes will be opened to see more than you ever expected about yourself—and God. Above all, our hope is that strongholds will be crushed, and the glory of God will bring dark places into the light.

While some of the women we've looked at turned away from God, most ran to Him. This is the secret of a joy-filled, victorious Christian life. We must run to God and throw ourselves into His arms every day— and if needed, every minute—so that we receive the strength, patience, and grace to live as His followers in this chaotic, broken world. Only then can we impart the grace we've been given. Only then will we find endurance and peace. We have heard it said, "God never wastes a hurt." Keep that in mind as you continue your journey. In time, someone will cross your path who has the same kind of wound you have, and they'll be desperately trying to find a way to soothe it. With greater empathy for the one who's hurting, you can assure them: "You are not alone."

When you do, you'll begin to reap the rewards that come from living victoriously. You'll see that by God's grace, your wounded places become ministry spaces.

We pray that you've found a greater purpose in your pain; that, like Abigail, you begin to value yourself more; like those in wounded relationships, you start to forgive others—and yourself—more; like Jochebed, you are willing to release and surrender more. We pray that like Ruth, you find the right path; like Martha and Mary, you begin to see God more; and like the widow of Zarephath, through Christ, you are fed, more and more.

Our lives will never be free of problems . . . but we *can* be free.

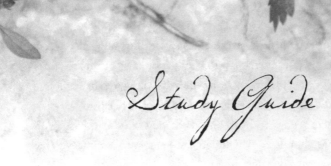

Study Guide

DEAR FRIENDS, OUR PRAYER is that this study guide will provide fresh insight into the book's chapters . . . and into your heart. Take time to invest in yourself *and* other women through this section. When we are wounded, our natural tendency is to hide those wounds from the world, and even ourselves. Let us encourage you to take charge of the wound, rather than the wound having complete control over you.

Healing takes place when we realize we are not alone. There's something therapeutic about a group of women who cry together, pray together, and encourage one another. (To all the women who have found freedom: what a great way to allow God to use you to minister to other women! Become a facilitator, spurring your friends on toward healing.) If you decide to go through the study guide as a group, please let us know. You can find our contact information in the back of the book. We'd love to have a Skype session with you, to meet the wonderful women you've gathered, and to help kick off your time together.

We have created questions related to each chapter for you to use during group or individual study. Our "Talk It Out" section features conversation starters related to the book (and related topics). It's a great way to get ladies talking and sharing—as well as learning from—their common life experiences.

Here's your chance to get honest and share wounds you've never shared before. (However, don't worry if you don't feel like talking in a group study. We know God will minister to you as you soak everything in.)

The "Hope for the Healing" section gives you short nuggets of truth to ponder, write in your journal, and/or talk about as a group.

Finally, the "Write It Out" section will help you work through your toughest issues. It will give you a chance to search the Scriptures, reflect on wounds, discuss ways to heal, and learn how God can carry you. We've also included prayers, which you can personalize. However, feel free to write and pray your own prayers.

We know this can all be a bit intimidating. We believe, however, that when your desire to be healed is strong enough to overcome your resistance to change, you will do whatever it takes to move forward. Jesus is asking you the same thing he asked the paralyzed man by the pool of Bethesda: "Do you want to get well?" (John 5:6)

You are the only person who can answer that question.

For those of you who feel you're "okay," we encourage you to go ahead and work through this study guide. You may be surprised to find you are still holding on to some wound, from which God wants to free you.

Things you'll need:

+ Bible (in a translation that is easy for you to understand)
+ Notebook or journal
+ Pen
+ And most important—transparency

Helpful Tips:

+ Create moments to pray for one another. There is power in prayer!
+ Remember—things shared in a group need to be kept in great confidence.
+ Make the group a safe place for everyone.

We pray you will find strength to climb mountains, speak profound words, and allow deeply buried tears to overflow. May your journey be successful. Let the healing begin—it's time.

Chapter One: Two Women in Solomon's Court

Talk It Out

1. Why do women create such unique bonds?
2. Think of a metaphor that might describe your relationship with a particular friend. Is it like a peanut butter and jelly sandwich or more like two slices of bread standing alone?
3. How can women continue to bond even though we are created so differently?
4. Without naming names, have you (or do you know of someone who has) been betrayed by a friend? Share. What steps were taken to heal? What steps can we take? Explain.
5. Read Matthew 26:14–25. Who was betrayed in this passage? How difficult do you suppose it was for Jesus, as Judas was not only His friend, but His follower?
6. How does it comfort you to know Jesus experienced betrayal as well?

Hope for the Healing

+ *Hurt people hurt people.* Remember when someone hurts you, they are probably hurting too.
+ You are only responsible for you.
+ "A gossip betrays a confidence; so avoid anyone who talks too much" (Prov. 20:19).

Write It Out

1. Read 1 Kings 3:19–28. List the losses women in the lesson faced. Name a loss you can relate to (loss of a friendship, loss of a child, loss of trust, etc.). Explain.
2. Which woman in the lesson do you empathize with the most? In what way?

3. Focus on your most hurtful moment involving a friend. What feelings surface at the thought of it? List them.

4. Read Colossians 3:12–14. What does the Scripture passage say we are to "clothe" ourselves with? How are we to forgive?

5. What is the one thing that will bind us together in unity? We may not be able to find a way on our own to love someone who has hurt us deeply—but if we walk in *God's* love and *His* ways, through Him we will be able to extend kindness, compassion, gentleness, and patience. And that is love.

6. Read 2 Corinthians 2:5–8. Some people will hold on to their bitterness and never forgive. The good news is, you get to choose! Paul wrote that we need to affirm our love for those who have harmed us, but we also need to affirm in ourselves the love Christ gives us— no matter our faults. Decide today what you truly want. Do you want to forgive? Do you long for forgiveness? Write it out.

> *Lord, I've been hurt. And though I know I need to forgive, I'm finding it so difficult. Give me the strength I need to let go of this pain. Help me to release the person who has hurt me into Your care. I can't do it on my own, Lord, so I'm trusting in You to come alongside me. Heal me of the bitterness I feel, and forgive me of my anger and the grudge I've carried too long. I know that You've forgiven me much more than I can even imagine. Cleanse me and make me clean. Thank You for Your grace and mercy, which is boundless, and help me to grow more loving— more like You—each day. Amen.*

Chapter Two: Abigail

Talk It Out

1. What do you love about Abigail?
2. Talk about her strengths.
3. Talk about her weaknesses.
4. In what ways can you relate to Abigail?
5. Think about her courage, personality, and boldness. Ponder her peacemaking skills. Discuss.
6. How are you different from Abigail? How are you like her?
7. Take a moment to discuss the many different types of abuse.
8. How can abuse strip away everything good and lovely in a woman?
9. What steps can a woman take to rebuild her self-esteem, confidence, and self-worth?

Hope for the Healing
+ Remember—God *is* with you.
+ You are not the cause of the abuse!
+ You deserve respect, admiration, and value.

Write It Out

1. In what way did Abigail help her husband continue his destructive behavior? Explain.
2. Abigail responded a certain way to her husband's behavior. How would you define your temperament and behavior when faced with conflict—with your spouse or in another relationship?
3. God changed Abigail's life. You may not be able to marry a king, but you can express to God what areas of your relationships you would like to see changed. Write it out: "I would like . . ." "I desire to . . ." "I long for . . ."
4. Read 2 Corinthians 1:3–11. Paul praised the Father of _____

and the God of _____. What did Paul say about his suffering and abuse? What did Paul set his hope on?

5. When we have been abused, we forget how lovely we are—that God created us out of His own personal beauty. We forget that He knows our wounds, understands our hurts, and identifies the broken pieces of our soul. Though we feel alone—He is ever present. Read Psalm 139 as a reminder.

6. Later on we'll deal with God disappointing us, but for now—what hope does this passage give us?

> *Lord, though You sometimes seem far away, I thank You that You never leave my side. Open my eyes to see how much You love me. Help me to see the beauty in me You created. Pull out every lovely thing and make it visible before my eyes. My desire is to humbly love myself as much as You love me. Place a shield of protection around me. Give me a clear direction for my life. Give me the courage to take the steps I need to move toward healing, knowing You will walk with me. I need You Lord, I need You. Amen.*

Chapter Three: Dinah

Talk It Out

1. As with Jacob's family, sometimes our journeys can lead us to places we least expect. Share an experience, good or bad. What lessons did you come away with from that experience?

2. Like Dinah, many women get lost in their abuse, their journey, and in the violation. Take a moment and discuss why that might happen.

3. Has an issue with abuse kept you from pursuing a dream or moving forward into something you really wanted to do? Explain.

4. What steps can we take in helping others who have experienced a loss to find help, hope, and healing?

5. Think of a time when another Christian woman encouraged you, kept your secret, or walked with you. How did it impact you? How did it strengthen you?

Hope for the Healing

+ Decide you want to get better.
+ Turn your powerlessness into praise. Seek help!
+ Though others may help, God is the only One who can set us free.

Write It Out

1. Dinah experienced an incredibly vile act. Have you (or do you know of someone who) experienced such an act as Dinah? Explain.

2. Who or what do you turn to when emotions surface and you find yourself struggling?

3. Is it difficult to turn to God when you're hurting? If so, why? What makes some situations more difficult than others?

4. As with Dinah's brothers, our hurt turned inward can result in

hate. Read 1 John 2:8–10. Where are you living—in the light or in the darkness?

5. Read Isaiah 43:1–3. Change the words "Jacob" and "Israel" to your name. God promises to be with us in our suffering and sorrows. We may not always be spared—but He promises to walk through it with us. How does this passage make you feel (disappointed, hurt, angry, hopeful, protected, encouraged)? Why? Write it out—get to the heart of your emotions.

6. Isaiah 63:9 says, "In all their distress [God] too was distressed." Do you think God hurts when we hurt?

7. Read Psalm 106:44–45. Name four things God did, according to the psalmist, which He can do for us. (*Relented*, in Hebrew, means "comforted.")

(A prayer for anyone violated by sexual abuse)

Lord, I have been [name how you've been wounded in this way]. My heart and soul cry out to You. I don't know what to do with this pain. I feel [list your emotion about it and toward God]. I'm trying to [name how you are trying to heal]. My mind churns with the memory and emotion. Cleanse me of those wounded memories and free me from the stronghold of the wound. Lead me to the water that cleanses my spirit, refreshes my soul, and flows over my body. I surrender my suffering to You, Lord. I surrender my pain to You. I surrender Lord—to You. I no longer want, need, or desire to hold on to my pain. Help me as I take steps toward healing. May this day, this moment, become the beginning of freedom for me. I thank You, Lord, for what You are about to do in my life. Amen.

Chapter Four: Ruth

Talk It Out

1. In what ways does your life mirror Ruth's? (For example, did you grow up without knowing the one true God, experience a wonderful relationship with your mother-in-law, lose a spouse before having children, come to know God through your husband's family, have to work as a single woman to provide for yourself, etc.?)
2. Would you have moved your family to a place like Moab? Can you relate? Examine the benefits and liabilities.
3. How is today's world similar to that of Ruth's?
4. Discuss the relationships daughters-in-law have with mothers-in-law.
5. What do you love about Ruth and Naomi's relationship?
6. What created their bond and love for one another?

> ### Hope for the Healing
> - Allow yourself to journey through the stages of grief.
> - Don't camp out in a grief stage and not move forward.
> - Trust that God still has an amazing journey for your life.

Write It Out

1. Have you (or do you know of someone who has) lost a spouse? How did it impact you or your friend? Go deep; pull out those deep-seated emotions.
2. There are many ways we experience grief besides losing a loved one. In what way(s) have you experienced grief (a move to a new city, the

loss of a friendship, death of a loved one, loss of a job, issues with finances, loss of a home, etc.)?

3. What stage of grief would you consider yourself in today (denial, anger, bargaining, depression, acceptance)? How were you able to move through the stages of grief? If you are camped out in a particular grief stage other than 5 (acceptance), why do you suppose you are having trouble moving forward?

4. Read Lamentations 3:32–33. What does the writer say about God? Now read Psalm 71:19–21. What does the psalmist say about God? How does this bring hope to your life?

5. Read Nehemiah 2:1–3. What was Nehemiah grieving?

6. The city, Jerusalem, had been destroyed by the Babylonians. Besides losing their homes, many Israelites lost family members through death and captivity. Nehemiah rebuilt the city and brought back the people. Read Nehemiah 8:2–12. What encouragement did Nehemiah give the people? List those things we can hold on to in order to sustain us through our grieving process. How does understanding the Word of the Lord help us journey through grief?

> Jesus, I'm hurting. It seems as if life is full of loss, and it's hard to hold on to hope. I know You are a Man of sorrows, acquainted with grief. Thank You for becoming fully human so that You could share in our pain. Give me Your peace and perspective today. Show me the hope I have in You, through the cross of Christ. Even as I look forward to an eternity with You and those I love, help me to live each day fully and appreciate the gifts of ordinary days. Be my all in all, Lord—the One who will never leave me or forsake me. Amen.

Chapter Five: Hagar

Talk It Out

1. Take a moment and try to empathize with Hagar's wounds. How do you suppose she felt as a slave in Abraham's family? What do you think the friction between her and Sarah was about?

2. Can you relate to Hagar moving from a city she was probably raised in to a new area with a different culture, where they served a God her people didn't worship?

3. If you moved, especially if those moves were frequent, what wounds did you experience from being relocated?

4. The world can be a cruel place in which to live. Hagar's experience with Sarah was not so different from what many of today's women face. Have you found yourself in a situation like Hagar, where you worked under the authority of someone who mistreated you? Did you leave like Hagar did, or did you stay? How did you handle the situation?

5. Hagar experienced a moment where God revealed Himself to her. She said, "I have now seen the God who sees me." Share an experience where God revealed Himself to you. If you haven't had that kind of experience, ask God to meet you in a personal way.

6. What insight did you gain from that experience? Or what do you hope to gain from a future experience?

Hope for the Healing

- The God who sees you also sees your wounded heart.
- "In faithfulness he will bring forth justice" (Isa. 42:3).
- "Wait in hope for the LORD; he is our help and our shield" (Ps. 33:20).

Write It Out

1. We've all been mistreated at some point in our lives. Write about your earliest memory of being mistreated. How old were you? Where did it happen? Who wounded you? List the feelings that surface when you recall that moment.

2. Take a moment and write about your most *recent* memory of being mistreated. List the feelings that surface when you recall that moment.

3. Compare your feelings from your earliest memory to those from your most recent. Which emotions are the same? Which are different?

4. When we are mistreated, it shakes the very core of our hearts, and we may feel as if God isn't near. But He is. Read Isaiah 41:8–10. Insert your name in the place of "Israel." List two things God reveals about you from this verse. List two other things He promises to do.

5. When we feel mistreated, emotions from past wounds can sometimes surface. But God wants to change us. He wants to strengthen and heal us so we can have emotional health and maturity. Read Romans 14:8–14. How does Paul say we should behave? What will provide our strength to make those choices?

> *Dear God, I don't have the strength to carry [insert the emotions you listed above] anymore. I thank You for helping me work through [name the emotions again]. I lay my most intimate feelings at Your feet, trusting You will know what to do with them. Restore my heart, Lord, and help me to find forgiveness. I'm ready to receive Your healing power. I need it, Lord. I need You! Thank You. In Jesus's precious name. Amen.*

Chapter Six: Jochebed

Talk It Out

1. Jochebed came up with a clever plan for releasing her child. Talk about some creative ways parents can release their children in today's world, ways that allow kids to experience and investigate their surroundings in a positive manner.

2. How can we build confidence and esteem in children before releasing them?

3. How does our confidence line up with God's confidence concerning our children? Can we trust God's care more than ours?

4. Talk about the difficulties women especially face in releasing their children.

5. Why does the way we release them make a difference?

6. What encouragement can we give other women who might be having a difficult time letting go?

7. What part of Jochebed's story can you relate to? Share.

8. Name one point in her story that stood out to you.

Hope for the Healing

+ Before you knew your child, God formed him or her in your womb.
+ Believe it or not, God is more invested in your child than you are.
+ Enjoy each stage of parenthood, and try to stay in the moment with your kids (it's hard, we know!).

Write It Out

1. There are many ways parents (or others) can release a child. Read Genesis 22:1–12. In what way did Abraham release his son Isaac?

2. Read 1 Samuel 1:21–28. What gave Hannah the strength to let go of Samuel?

3. Describe a moment when you, or someone you know, had to release a child. What were the circumstances? How were you, or they, able to work through the emotions involved?

4. Reflect on Mary, the mother of Jesus. What difficulties did she endure in letting her son go? What were the benefits in her surrendering Him?

5. What is your greatest fear in letting a child go? Though it is hard to fathom, releasing our children to God may be the best thing we could ever do. Think about Jochebed releasing Moses. With deep groaning from a heart saturated in grief she did what seemed impossible. What was the end result?

> *Father, I long to hold on to the child You have given me. My heart aches at the very thought of having to release him/her. In my mind of confusion and want, I cannot fathom the thought of having to trust so deeply—so I ask for Your help, Lord. Release me, Father—so that I can release my child. Help me to understand that he/she is never far away. Open my eyes to see that You love him/her far more than I could comprehend. Give me strength to let go of the things I need to let go of, and provide Your peace as I reflect back on my most cherished moments with him/her. I praise You, Lord, for the work You are going to do in the midst of the sorrow. Amen.*

Chapter Seven: Mary & Martha

Talk It Out

1. Would you consider yourself to be a "Martha" or a "Mary"? Share.
2. Discuss the positives and negatives of having each perspective.
3. Describe a moment when you faced disappointment with God.
4. What causes us to turn *away* from God during disappointments?
5. What causes us to turn *toward* God during disappointments?
6. How do you feel about Mary's courageous act with Jesus? What comes to mind (repentance, worship, honor, etc.)?
7. What message can you take away from Mary's and Martha's experiences?

> ### Hope for the Healing
> + God does not abandon us!
> + His ways, not the world's, are holy—though we may not understand them.
> + His desire is to reveal Himself to us in amazing ways.

Write It Out

1. In "Talk It Out," you were asked to share an experience of being disappointed in God. Now write it out. What was your most wounded moment of being disappointed in God? How did you really feel about it?
2. Did the experience cause distance or closeness with God? Why?
3. We often expect God to do certain things in our lives and perform in a certain way. What are some of your expectations of God?
4. How has God not met your expectations of Him?
5. Read John 11:38–45. What was Jesus trying to reveal to Martha and Mary by waiting to come when they called for Him? Do you

suppose God might be trying to reveal something in the midst of your disappointments?

6. We may not understand everything God does, but we can have full confidence in Him. Read Psalm 27:13–14. What did the psalmist ask us to do? Read Psalm 130:5–6. Can you hear the urgency of the psalmist? What did the psalmist put his hope in?

7. Read Jeremiah 17:5–8. Describe the visual picture Jeremiah painted for those who trust and wait in the Lord. How does this bring comfort and hope to you?

> *Heavenly Father, I don't always understand Your ways or timing. Forgive me for not trusting You, and thank You for the compassion You have on me. Help me release my expectations and plans into Your hands, knowing that You care more about me than I could ever imagine. Amen.*

Chapter Eight: Wounded Relationships

Talk It Out

1. Discuss the chapter. What impacted you the most?
2. Which couple from this chapter, do you relate to—Adam and Eve, Ahab and Jezebel, Hosea and Gomer, or others? Explain.
3. What do you feel is the biggest issue facing marriages today?
4. If you feel comfortable, share what has been the most difficult struggle in your marriage, or relationship. (Please keep the focus on you.)
5. What steps can we take to find healing in our marriages or dating relationships?
6. How can we encourage, help, and walk with other women facing issues in their marriages or relationships? (Be specific.)

> ### Hope for the Healing
> + A tapestry of shame is something the enemy, not God, wants you to wear.
> + Jesus is coming with healing in His wings (Mal. 4:2)!
> + "Though your sins are like scarlet, they shall be as white as snow" (Isa. 1:18).

Write It Out

1. Have you been, or are you now, in a relationship? How would you describe it?
2. Did you identify with any of the stories or relationships in this chapter? Which one? How? Explain.
3. What is the most difficult struggle in your relationship? Blaming is easy. It is more difficult to get real with ourselves and how we are feeling.

4. Read Psalm 133. The oil symbolizes the Holy Spirit. Imagine you and your spouse, or the one you are dating, standing before the Lord. Now, picture the Lord pouring oil upon the two of you. See it run down your heads, onto your clothes, and down to your feet. Read the Psalm again and replace the word "people" with your names. What is God saying to you?

5. "The LORD bestows his blessing, even life forevermore" (v. 3). In the Hebrew the word "bestows" means "commanded"—*tsavah*—which means to "give charge—give orders." In other words when we make an effort to join together in unity, God makes an effort to "order" His blessings over us. What an amazing thing to ponder—He orders the blessings! What would this mean to you?

> *Father, I offer my relationship to You. Forgive us, restore us, create in us a clean heart and renew a right spirit within us. Bring healing to our lives, Lord. Comfort us. Mend our wounds. Help us to yield ourselves to You. Please become the center of our relationship. I praise You for the great things You are going to do. Amen.*

Chapter Nine: Weary, Wanting Women

Talk It Out

1. Talk about the women in the chapter who could not conceive a child. Which woman's story in the chapter touched you the most? Why?

2. How difficult do you suppose barrenness was, especially in that culture? Why was it important? Why do women long to conceive in today's culture? Talk about the difference.

3. Have you struggled, or do you know of another woman's struggle, to have a child? Share the emotions involved with that wound.

4. What encouragement have you been given by other women regarding this issue? Was it helpful or hurtful? What encouragement have you given other women? Do you think what you said was hurtful or helpful?

5. Read Isaiah 54:1–2. Discuss your interpretation of the passage. What stands out? What specific words might give hope to barren women?

Hope for the Healing

+ God is still very near . . . and still very much in love with you.
+ God will birth something out of you, if you let Him, though it may not be what you expect.
+ God will heal and soothe your aching heart—if you will allow Him to.

Write It Out

1. Write about whether you had difficulty with conception and/or whether you were able to conceive a child. Go deep—really pull out those buried emotions. Are you able to have any more children? Why or why not?

2. How do you feel about God—right now—regarding your situation? What changes in your heart would you like to see?

3. Do you believe God could birth something in you other than a child? How do you feel about that? Would it be difficult to accept His offering if it is *not* a child? Why or why not?

4. Read Psalm 113:4–9. What does this passage mean to you? Are you able to apply it to your life? Why or why not?

5. *Infertility* is a word that causes emotions to surface. Sometimes it's difficult to sort through our feelings when we've been so wounded. Take a moment and write it out. God does care. He is present. Take courage. He will comfort.

> *Lord, I've tried and nothing happens. My wounds feel*
> _____. *Lord, I hurt, I ache, and I despair.*
> *Come and heal* _____. *Lord, when I see my*
> *friends having babies it feels like* _____.
> *Lord, when others try to help, they say* _____.
> *But I need* _____. *Lord, I've endured tests, doc-*
> *tor visits, and difficulties. Is there a way for You to redeem*
> *my pain and transform it? Reveal to me the changes You*
> *are making in my life. I need* _____.
> *Lord, give me wisdom and guidance in the path I should*
> *take. Lord, fill the empty hole in my heart with* _____
> _____. *Give me strength, Lord, to* _____.
> *In Jesus' name. Amen.*

Chapter Ten: Ichabod's Mother

Talk It Out

1. Share what impacted you the most about Ichabod's story.

2. Have you experienced similar wounds? Share.

3. In what ways can you *specifically* relate to Ichabod's mother's story—whether from her actions or others? (For instance, have you married into a pastoral family, endured the embarrassment of a spouse's behavior, ignored ongoing sin in your family, chosen not to discipline your children, cursed God, etc.?)

4. Sometimes we experience wound after wound, causing sorrow and hurt to pile upon us. Share about a season when you experienced trial after trial. How did you cope and find hope? Was God revealed through your suffering? How?

5. Think about God's glory. For God to reveal His glory, He sent His Son to us in visible form. How was God's glory revealed through Jesus?

6. What did Ichabod's mother miss out on when she cursed God?

Hope for the Healing

+ God is still in charge.
+ Sometimes our greatest attributes come from traveling through trials.
+ "Pain doesn't sideline us unless we let it."

Write It Out

1. Our seasons of trials and tribulations come and go. Reflect back on a season where you felt you almost couldn't make it. Write about the emotions of the wound. How did it impact you? Change your life?

2. How did you manage to get through the storm? What sustained you during that time?

3. Was it difficult to draw close to God? If so, why? If not, how did it draw you closer to Him?

> For his Holy Spirit speaks to us deep in our hearts and tells us we are God's children. And since we are his children, we will share his treasures—for everything God gives to his Son, Christ, is ours, too. But if we are to share his glory, we must also share his suffering. Yet what we suffer now is nothing compared to the glory he will give us later. (Rom. 8:16–18 NLT 1996)

4. Ichabod's mother, in her suffering, declared that the glory of God departed; that there was no glory. How does this Scripture speak to you regarding your own suffering—as well as God's glory?

5. Read Romans 8:26–28. What happens when we have no idea how to pray or what to pray for in our moments of turmoil? What encourages you the most about this passage?

> *Father, this season of suffering seems unbearable. When will your warm light shine upon me? Life at times appears unfair. Help me to see that you still love me, delight in me, and embrace me. I need you, Lord, to help me through this tiring time. Give me strength to endure—to rise up with faith that you are still a God who sees. Remind me of your strength and control. Come and comfort me, Lord. Seal and bind my wounds. Lavish me with your abundant blessings. May this season pass, I ask and pray. Amen.*

Chapter Eleven: Jephthah's Daughter

Talk It Out

1. Discuss the relationship daughters have with their fathers.
2. How did you see your father when you were a little girl? How do you see him today?
3. Describe a moment when you saw your father's imperfections for the very first time. How did it change your view of him? How were you able to cope with the realization that your father wasn't perfect?
4. Share a moment of being wounded by your father. What impacted you most about the wound? Did healing with your father occur? How? If not, why?
5. Share some of your most positive memories about your father.

> ### Hope for the Healing
> + Fathers are people too—made of flesh and blood; full of both praiseworthy and sinful attributes.
> + God is the *only* Father who will never fail us.
> + Find ways to share your life with your dad. You can set healthy boundaries and grab hold of those precious moments with your father—even if just for a few seconds.

Write It Out

1. Write about your most hurtful wound involving your father. Did he hurt you, or did you hurt him? How did it change your relationship? Was the relationship restored? If so, how? If not, why not?
2. Write about the wound of growing up without a father—either from loss, abandonment, or detachment. What impact has it had on your life?

3. How do you view God? Would you consider Him your Father? Why, or why not?

4. Sometimes it's difficult to view God as our Father *because* of our earthly fathers, but God is neither man nor woman—He is God. He loved us so much He sent His son, Jesus, to earth so that His (God's) face and actions might be revealed. Through Jesus, we can get a clear view of what a father should be. Examine these verses. Choose the ones you struggle with the most regarding your earthly father. Write a prayer to God, expressing your desire for a heavenly Father.

> Our heavenly Father is . . .
> **Love**—John 3:16
> **Trustworthy**—Numbers 23:19
> **Near Us**—Deuteronomy 4:7
> **Jealous for Us**—Deuteronomy 4:24
> **Merciful (Kind)**—Deuteronomy 4:31
> **Leader**—2 Chronicles 13:12
> **Full of Compassion**—Psalm 116:5
> **Forgiving**—Daniel 9:9
> **Wise**—1 Corinthians 1:25
> **Full of Blessings**—2 Corinthians 9:8

God, I know You are the perfect "Abba" (Daddy) that my father was unable to be for me. Help me to climb onto Your lap when I need soothing, instead of running to the world. Thank You for Your constant care and compassion. Help me to show that same love to my own father, recognizing how human and frail he is. Abba, Father, I love You with all my heart. Amen.

Chapter Twelve: The Widow of Zarephath

Talk It Out

1. How do you picture yourself in the midst of a crisis involving your circumstances? Wayward Worrier? Bellowing Believer? Reluctant Realist? Explain. How do you *desire* to respond?

2. What circumstances have you had to endure this past year? Did you try to take matters in your own hands, or did God send help? What was the result?

3. Would you receive help if offered, like the widow of Zarephath, or would you be reluctant? Share why it might be difficult for you to receive or ask for help.

4. Share a moment when you needed help and God provided.

> ### Hope for the Healing
> + God has heard your cry.
> + Trust that He is perfecting all good things.
> + Draw near to God—rest in Him.

Write It Out

1. Write about a circumstance that completely overwhelmed you. What was the greatest hardship in that circumstance?

2. Do you believe God was present? If not, why? If so, how?

3. Were you able to take any steps toward God during that time? Did you reach out to Him? If so, how? If not, why?

4. Read Genesis 22:13–14. Abraham went through a trying time when God asked him to sacrifice his son, but God intervened. What did Abraham say after God provided the ram?

5. With suffering, we often learn endurance and sacrifice. Suffering is like a yoke tightened around an oxen's neck. But God eventually breaks our yoke, and through Him, we find freedom. Read

Ezekiel 34:25–31. What is God saying in this passage? Will you claim it?

> *Dear Father, I come to You, broken and weary. I long for freedom and release from my dismal circumstance. Today, I claim this Scripture as a covenant and promise from You. Give me peace, shower Your blessings upon me, rescue me from those things that bind, and deliver me from evil. Take away the famine—feed me, Lord. Take away the drought—quench my thirst, Lord. I thank You that I can lay my head down in a safe and secure place. I am not afraid. I will wait for You. I will watch for You. I will trust in You. You are my God, and I praise You for taking care of me—Your child. In the name of the Most High King I pray. Amen.*

Acknowledgments

TINA ❀ My life has consisted of wounded years, days, and moments. I have been able to walk through some of those with little scarring, while others have left me in piles of pain and under mounds of mire. The good news is, like the psalmist said in chapter 40 verse 2, "[The Lord] lifted me out of the slimy pit, out of the mud and mire; he set my feet on a rock and gave me a firm place to stand." The Lord has become the greatest healer and friend I could ever want. He is the One my deepest thanks goes to. I will forever be grateful for His love and care.

Years ago, a lonely young pastor's wife walked into a production rehearsal and asked, "Is this seat taken?" The woman responded, "No, you can sit here." We've been sitting together ever since. Thank you, Dena, for your wonderful friendship, tears on the phone, prayers through email and beyond, and the amazing things you've taught me about writing. Though we're far away geographically, we are still ever-so-close. I love you, girl! Thank you for the terribly hard and strenuous work you put into the book. It was such an unbelievable experience, and something I will always treasure. I pray we write many more books together!

I also thank Greg and Becky Johnson for believing in this book. Greg, thank you for working hard as our agent to get the book sold, and for the prayers I know you put into it as well. Thank you, Kregel Publications, for giving our idea a chance. May you be greatly blessed because of it!

Thank you to my Grace River Church family for the gracious encouragement, support, and affection you've shown by tending to my family's wounds. We feel loved and nurtured by your acts of kindness and your genuine display of Christ's character. You are truly jewels of grace, and we love you so much!

To the wounded friends who have entrusted me with your deepest secrets, pain, and despair: I am honored and blessed to have had a chance to journey with you through your darkest times, and to see you come out on the other side—into the light of God's glorious healing. This book is so much about you, and for you. Thank you for allowing me to pray with you—and for you praying with me. I love you, ladies.

I have faced many wounds, but I've never been alone. My large family of eleven siblings has been the strength of my journey. Thank you, my sweet Kinsey Clan—and I mean the entire clan (aunts, uncles, nephews, and nieces)! Thank you, Mom (Faye); sisters Pam and Becky; sisters-in-law Karen, Jackie, Amber, and Debra; brothers David, Jimmy, Wayne, Gary, Michael, Rusty, Ronnie, and Kenneth; and my one and only brother-in-law, David; for weeping, crying, and praying with me through so much pain. Though we've had to hold back the shotguns a few times, you were always there to carry me through every crisis. I love you so much! And to my precious father-in-law, Ted Samples: I love you and thank you for praying me through this project!

Thank you, Tom Pals and Ken Datson, my counselors and friends, for your work, which helped open my eyes and heart to God's healing in such a unique way. You have seen mine, as well as David's, deepest wounds, allowed us to unload time and again, and brought such insight into our suffering. Truly, so much of my healing has come because of you—and I feel blessed you're in my life as well as David's.

Now, to my most precious family. There are times and moments when families wound each other. There are times when we desire to run away, forget about it, and stop growing together. Believe me, I have had moments like that. But I can honestly say, I am so thankful for the journey thus far. Every tear, painful memory, wavering thought, act of unkindness, and so much more, is nothing compared to the healing we've also experienced. I treasure your tears of empathy, unwavering commitment, words of kindness, acts of love. David, you are handsomely brilliant! Without you, I would have never made it past the first chapter. Thank you so much for your words of wisdom, witty phrases, and scholarly knowledge—and coming up with the title, *Wounded Women of the Bible*. I really do love you! Jaren, you have taught me so much about love and what it means to love unconditionally. I am in awe of your strength and willingness to soldier through your toughest wounds. Your talent and love for God shine bright and warm my heart so much. You are an inspiration, son, and I love you! Jillian, my precious daughter-in-law, my eyes have been opened to see your true beauty. I love watching you grow in Christ. I am proud to call you daughter! Zach, my strong warrior and fighter—one who rarely shows his hurts, physically or emotionally, yet gently embraces when it's needed, and always sees the good in others: when you do come to me with your wounds, I know you must really be hurting. I love that you still come. You are amazing, and I love you, son.

Praise God for His amazing work in our lives!

DENA ❧ Tina—we've been through a lot together, and I love you so much! Thank you for coming to me with this incredible, God-given idea . . . and for trusting me implicitly with it. I pray I've handled it in a worthy way. My dear friend, I've watched you live out what you've written in these pages, and you are a living testimony of God's healing. You inspire me with your wisdom, perseverance, generosity, and love for Jesus. Thank you for making this process such a pleasure. I agree— let's do it again.

Greg and Becky, thanks for your friendship and support. Your enthusiasm for the concept was a wind in my sails during a difficult season, and your encouragement throughout the process has been invaluable. I'm glad God put us together, and I hope we continue to work (and play!) together for many years.

Kregel Publications, thank you for taking a chance on *Wounded Women of the Bible.* I love your heart for sharing biblically based resources with those who need them most. We are so thrilled to be on your team.

To my prayer team, Lakeside Baptist Church family, and dear friends (especially the Chick Posse, Frio Sisters, and my fellow High Calling editors)—thank you for your prayers, words of support, and the love you freely pour out. Like Moses's friends did for him, you hold up my arms when I'm too weak to go on. I am such a blessed woman to have you in my life.

To the women who shared their stories with us (and allowed us to share them with the world): *thank you.* We are honored and humbled. I pray we've represented you well.

To Nancy and Terry, my in-laws, and Marty and Malesa, my brother and sister-in-law, as well as Justin, Kaylen, and Lauren (and the entire Dyer family): I am grateful and humbled to be a part of your lives, and I hope you know how much you mean to me.

Mom and Dad, thanks for all the phone calls, shopping trips, cards, lunches, and "now, now, there, there" back rubs you gave me during one of the hardest times in my adult life. I am so glad we lived close together for a while. Thank you for a lifetime of sharing your love, faith, support, and selves so freely (and for still talking to me after I write about you).

Will and Julie, Molly and Noah: How I treasure our holidays (and ordinary days) together—in Amarillo, Granbury, and on Hay Creek Ranch. Thanks for your constant, unconditional support. My love for you is beyond words. Miss you like crazy!

To my sons: no mom could be prouder or more thankful than I am.

Jordan, what a strong, godly young man you're turning into! Thanks for your steady, calm presence in our home, and for encouraging me as I dove deep into this project. I love seeing your sense of humor and artistic talents blossom, and can't wait to see what God does with your multitude of gifts. Jackson, you have a heart as big as Texas and a personality to match. Thank you for being proud of Mommy, making me laugh, hugging me when I'm sad, and affirming me with your sweet words. You are a treasure!

To my husband, Carey: seventeen years has flown by, hasn't it? I treasure all of it—the good, bad, and in between. You are still my best friend, and the best husband and ministry partner anyone could ask for. I am so glad our sons are growing up with your zest for life, servant heart, and love for the Lord. Your giftedness amazes me, and your humility inspires me. Thank you for taking the boys on "guy-day Fridays" as I completed the book; for hugging me and praying for me when I fell apart during the process; and for wearing the mantle of "writer spouse"—and all that entails—with patience, humor, and grace. My life is so much richer because you are in it! You have my heart forever.

Finally, to my heavenly Father, thank You for calling me into Your ministry and for the work You've done in my life. Through the mercy and grace of Your Son, Jesus, the Great Physician, and the precious comfort and wisdom of your Holy Spirit, I've experienced a depth of healing and a richness of love that can't be described in words. However, I will spend my life trying to do just that. Thank You for the gift of writing and the amazing privilege of sharing it with others—this is all for You.

About the Authors

DENA DYER ❧ As a busy mom and minister's wife, Dena Dyer constantly loses things—but she's holding on to her sanity (barely). Her favorite forms of therapy? Talking and laughing with her sons, date nights with her hubby, reading, cooking, and watching movies. Dena is thankful for her creative life, which is varied and full. That doesn't mean it's easy, though.

"Jesus truly is my strength when I am weak," she says. "His love, mercy, and grace have been incredibly healing in my life. That's why I'm so passionate about sharing Him with others." In between helping her boys with homework and shuttling them to school and music lessons, she writes, speaks, and participates in the music and women's ministries at Lakeside Baptist Church in Granbury, Texas, where her husband serves as the worship and music minister.

Dena's publishing credits include *Let the Crows' Feet and Laugh Lines Come*, *Mothers of the Bible*, The Groovy Chicks' Road Trip series, and *Grace for the Race: Meditations for Busy Moms*. Her articles have appeared in *Writer's Digest*, *Woman's World*, *Home Life*, and many other magazines, and her tips have been published in *Working Mother*, *Thriving Family*, *Redbook*, *Family Circle*, *Parenting*, *Nick Jr.*, and *Scholastic Parent*.

Dena currently serves as a contributing editor with The High Calling (www.highcalling.org). Visit her website/blog, "Mother Inferior," (www.denadyer.com) or connect with her on Facebook (DenaDyerAuthor) or Twitter (motherinferior2).

TINA SAMPLES ❧

Tina Samples is a Colorado-based writer, speaker, and worship leader. She keeps busy serving alongside her husband, Dave, who is the lead pastor at Grace River Church in Windsor, Colorado (www.chasingrace.org).

As a Texas gal, Tina loves going "home" for the opportunity to hang with her family, the Kinsey clan. She spends quite a bit of time at baseball games watching her oh-so-grown-up son, Zach, play ball. (She dreads the day he will leave for college.) Tina's oldest son, Jaren, is married to Navy gal Jillian, and they live in California. Both of her sons are incredibly gifted musicians, and Tina is proud to have led worship with them.

Tina also loves photography, music, and teaching. Tina says, "The Lord is an amazing God of blessings. I feel so privileged when I get to speak or lead worship at women's retreats, conferences, or other events. More than anything, I love ministering to other women."

Tina's publishing credits include *Guideposts*; *Extraordinary Answers to Prayer: In Times of Change and Unexpected Answers*; *Angels, Miracles, and Heavenly Encounters: Real Life Stories of Supernatural Events*; and *The One Year Life Verse Devotional*. She has also contributed to *The Secret Place* devotional magazine, as well as *Quiet Hour* magazine. Her articles about music therapy have appeared in the *Colorado Baptist News*.

Join Tina online at www.tinasamples.com or link with her via Facebook (TinaSampleswriter) or Twitter (tinasamples).